Advanced Techniques in Data Communications

ALSO BY RALPH GLASGAL

Basic Techniques in Data Communications,
Artech House

Advanced Techniques in Data Communications

Ralph Glasgal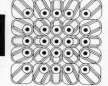

Artech House

Acknowledgments

The author gratefully acknowledges the contributions and comments made by the following individuals, who generously shared their substantial experience in the data communications field:

Plato Demos, Union Carbide; Jim Nichols, University of Colorado; Gary McConnell, University of Pennsylvania; Larry Roland, A.G. Edwards; and James Brennan, Interactive Services.

Foreword

The last decade has seen an unprecedented expansion of computerized services and systems whose feasibility depends on long-distance communications. Centralized billing, order entry, and inventory control systems, to mention just a few applications, are practical only if data can be quickly passed between remote points of the system and the central data bank. Remote timesharing service allows even small businesses to have real-time access to the programs and capabilities of very large computers via data communications networks.

Even though the well-established voice network of the Bell System has so far managed to accommodate the burgeoning need for data communications circuits, recent FCC decisions permitting the establishment of competitive digital transmission networks and specialized data services by the Bell System have made available new and more extensive transmission facilities at much lower cost. The new all-digital facilities have already demonstrated that they can deliver data over great distances with negligible error rates. The combination of low cost and high transmission quality should encourage the development of systems formerly considered marginal, either technically or economically.

In order to take full advantage of the facilities that are available, devices such as multiplexers and data concentrators are required. Most of the new digital networks use multiplexers in their internal transmission hierarchies; many customers, though, are finding that substantial savings can be achieved by multiplexing or concentrating on site before going on to a digital transmission circuit. This book is designed to assist communications system managers and designers in optimizing their configurations. Several types of multiplexers are discussed, as are inverse multiplexers, channel contention units, frequency division multiplexers, and standard interfaces.

Ralph Glasgal
Old Tappan, New Jersey

Table of Contents

Advanced Techniques in Data Communications

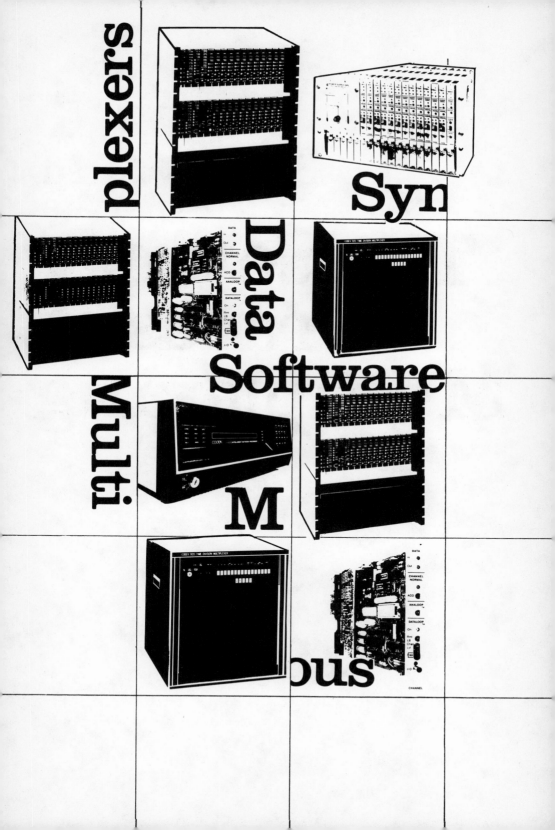

The Saving Graces of Multiplexing

The Saving Graces of Multiplexing

WHY MULTIPLEX?

Digital data multiplexers were invented to save money. They usually make it possible to save very large amounts of money and often pay for themselves in less than three or four months. The savings are realized primarily through the reduction of the number of transmission lines required to transmit a given number of data channels. Additional savings that can be achieved by multiplexing include a reduction in the amount of peripheral hardware, such as modems and computer front-end ports, and the substitution of leased-line facilities for the dial-up network.

A multiplexer is a hardware box consisting of central common logic and a variable number of channel cards. The process of multiplexing is simply the combining of several signal channels to form one composite data stream. Demultiplexing is the reconstitution of the original signal channels from the aggregate. That multiplexing is possible at all is due to the fact that the digital data channels normally used in communication systems have a greater capacity for transmitting data than do many of the terminals which are connected to them. A typical example is the ordinary voice line, either dedicated or dial-up — it has a bandwidth of about 3000 Hz, and yet it may be connected to a terminal such as the Teletype model 33, transmitting at a maximum rate of 110 baud. (In this book the term "baud" is used to define the signalling rate of asynchronous terminals and includes all the signalling elements, such as start, data, parity, and stop bits. All synchronous data streams, regardless of format, are assumed to contain only data information bits or characters; therefore, the term "bits per second" is used.) In the last ten years, the development of multilevel encoding techniques in modems has made commonplace the transmission of data at rates such as 4800, 7200, and 9600 bps; this improvement has enhanced the value of multiplexing techniques and, in particular, has given a boost to time division multiplexing at the expense of

1

the older frequency division multiplexing method. FDM is an analog technique and the sum of the bandwidths of each channel and the required guard bands between them cannot exceed the total bandwidth of the channel, which, in the case of voice-grade phone lines, is less than 3000 Hz. Typically, some eighteen teletypes can be frequency multiplexed, compared to 116 teletypes when using advanced modem and TDM equipment. In the future, however, the major disadvantage of FDM will be that a frequency division multiplexer generates tones and is therefore incompatible with the new all-digital transmission networks.

How Multiplexers Save Money

Figure 1-1 shows one of the simplest applications for multiplexers and illustrates how multiplexing can save such large sums of money. In the system of Figure 1-1(a), five IBM 2741's in one office in San Francisco communicate with five computer front-end ports in New York. By using a multiplexer as shown in Figure 1-1(b), four telephone lines have been eliminated. Since the cost of these lines would be approximately $2000 per month, a total saving of $8000 each month is achieved — enough money to pay for the multiplexer in the first month. Furthermore, instead of the ten modems previously required, only two are now needed. If one of the new digital network lines is used, even these modems would not be required and the saving would be even greater.

Intangible savings are the simplicity of the cabling and the convenience of the centralized diagnostic control that a multiplexer can offer. A later chapter on software multiplexing illustrates how further economies can be achieved through special software programming techniques.

Time Division Multiplexing Fundamentals

Time division multiplexing is a method of transmitting several messages on the same circuit by interleaving them in time. A time division multiplexer apportions all the bits available on an aggregate transmission line to the many slower

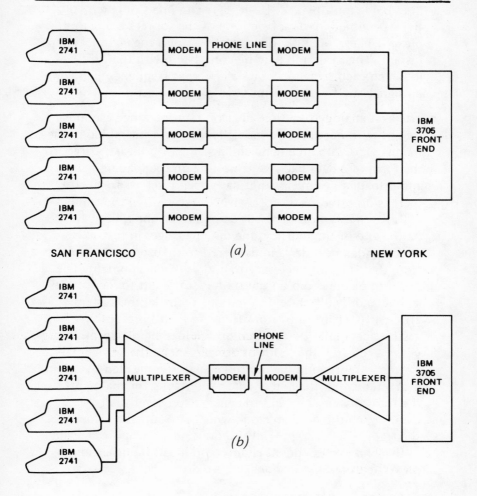

Figure 1-1/Multiplexers Save Money by Reducing Line and Modem Costs

3

lines being multiplexed. Each aggregate line slot is sequen-
tially occupied by data from one of the sources being multiplexed. Therefore only one signal occupies the channel at any
instant. This situation may be contrasted with that in FDM,
in which each signal occupies a different frequency band and
all signals are being transmitted simultaneously. (See Chapter 9)

The best analogy to a time division multiplexing system is a
freight train network. Periodically a train is assembled in the
freight yard with an engine and a string of boxcars. Cargo in
the form of a data package is waiting on the loading platform
and is loaded in boxcars that have been reserved for it. If
there is no cargo ready for a given boxcar when the train
pulls in, that boxcar goes out empty when the train leaves.
At the end of the journey, the data packages in the boxcars
are unloaded in order and delivered to their proper recipients.
Note that it is not necessary to address each shipment. The
position of the cargo on the train is sufficient to identify its
source and its ultimate destination. To make the system work
efficiently, trains must run often enough to prevent an excessive accumulation of cargo on the loading platform, but
yet not so often that a lot of boxcars make the trip empty.
The train represents the multiplexer frame (headed by a sync
character rather than an engine); the tracks are analogous to
the transmission line; and the energy to power the train
comes from the modem clock which also sets the velocity of
the train. The analogy is a valid one and we will use it again
in this and in subsequent chapters to illustrate other multiplexer features and options.

Asynchronous Data Multiplexing
Asynchronous data is defined as data from terminals that
generate start-stop characters; Teletype models 28 through
40 and the IBM 2741 are just such terminals. They generate
a character preceded by a start bit and concluded by stop

4

bits. The job of an asynchronous data multiplexer is to recognize such characters and assemble them into an aggregate high-speed data stream for transmission over a line to a demultiplexer which reverses the process. Figure 1-1(b) shows a typical basic system.

For reference purposes, Table 1-1 is a list of the asynchronous data speeds, formats, and character rates found in the normal multiplexing environment. TDM's must be capable of handling almost any combination of these speeds and codes.

Bit- vs. Character-Interleaved Multiplexers

In assembling a multiplexer train, the question arises as to what size to make the boxcars. The bigger they are, the more time it takes to collect a unit of cargo to fill one, and therefore the longer the delay in completing a shipment. But if the boxcars are too small, we may have to disassemble the cargo in order to load it into the car. To reassemble the cargo, we must send assembly instructions with it; these instructions take boxcars of their own, take time to interpret, and decrease shipping efficiency.

The usual choice is between using character- or bit-sized boxcars, and the decision is not an obvious one. In a character multiplexer, each boxcar is exactly one character in size. In a bit-interleaved multiplexer, each boxcar holds only one bit of a character, but extra bits have to be sent in order to know how to assemble the characters from these bits — so bit-interleaved TDM's are almost always faster but less efficient than their character-interleaved relatives. In general, multiplexing by character permits more non-data bits, such as the start and stop bits, to be stripped from incoming characters prior to multiplexing.

In an asynchronous character demultiplexer, a character is offloaded intact and then is packaged easily for local delivery with a start and the required number of stop bits. It is clear

Data Rate (Baud)	Equivalent in Characters per Second	Number of Data Bits	Type of Parity Bit	Minimum Number of Rest Bits	Code Name
50	6.67	5	none	1.5	Baudot
75	10	5	none	1.5	Baudot
110	10	7	even	2	ASCII
134.5	15	6	odd	1	IBM
150	15	7	even	1	ASCII
200	20	7	even	1	ASCII
300	30	7	even	1	ASCII
600	60	7	even	1	ASCII
600	66.6	6	odd	1	IBM
1050	140	5	none	1.5	Baudot
1200	120	7	even	1	ASCII
1200	171	5	none	1	Baudot

Table 1-1/Most Common Asynchronous Character Codes, Speeds, and Formats

where the start and stop bits should be inserted because each character arrives on the train as a discrete entity. In the bit-interleaved approach, it is necessary for the freight handler to keep a count of the bits received and to add the start and stop bits periodically where they belong. But he must be told where to start counting, which effectively means an extra bit must be sent; what is easier and more commonly done is to multiplex the start bit with the data bits.

Bit-interleaved TDM's require less storage (smaller loading platforms and lighter trains) and are better suited to synchronous data multiplexing; for asynchronous data, though, the bit-interleaving technique usually lacks both efficiency and option flexibility, and is not suitable for use in intelligent or software multiplexing systems (see Chapters 6 and 7). In most of the discussion that follows, character interleaving is assumed.

There are two major types of systems in which the shorter delay of a bit-interleaved TDM is a critical factor — Telex and Echoplexing. In the case of Telex channel multiplexing, a rapid transmission of call setup signals, such as "Proceed to Dial" pulses, is essential, lest their late arrival be misinterpreted as "Trunk Busy" or "Disconnect" signals. Typical character-interleaved multiplexers have delays about twice as long as can be tolerated by most existing Telex networks. Both frequency division multiplexers and bit-interleaved time division multiplexers are fast enough to be used in Telex systems without ill effect. The bit-interleaved units can handle more channels but require special logic to first recognize and then multiplex and demultiplex Telex call setup signals which have unusual formats, such as dial pulses and busy signals.

In Echoplexing, an operator at a typewriter keyboard depresses a key. The character generated is sent to the computer, which returns an identical character to the typewriter for printing. The process of echoing each character provides a simple method of checking for errors in the data entry process. Normally the echo comes back so fast that the operator is not aware of the delay and can maintain a satisfactory data entry rhythm. When a TDM is interposed in such a system, an additional round-trip delay of as much as four character times is introduced (about .4 of a second) and some operators find this difficult to work with. FDM or bit-interleaved multiplexers work well in this environment. Local loopback options on character-interleaved units offer only a partial solution to this problem since, although the delay is eliminated, the error-checking feature is lost as well. Intelligent character-interleaved TDM's can offer minimum delay echoplexing with the error-checking feature and are described in a later chapter.

Maintaining Frame Synchronization

Frame synchronization is needed to maintain port-to-port multiplexer integrity and to define the character bytes. The synchronization system insures that what goes in on Channel One at one end comes out on Channel One at the other. There are non-dedicated systems where port-to-port integrity is not significant, since terminals being multiplexed identify themselves to the computer. But, in most systems, some means of maintaining channel order and detecting a slippage in sync (and regaining it if there is a loss) are necessary; in all systems, character integrity is essential.

Returning to the train analogy — in order to avoid the necessity of putting address labels on each piece of cargo or sending bills of lading with each train, the source and destination of the cargo in each boxcar is preordained by the position of the boxcar in the train (counting from the engine). Trains are recognizable because each has an engine at its head. It would be quite wasteful if trains set out only occasionally, so on the multiplexer freight line, trains run continuously, caboose touching engine. With trains and freight cars continuously arriving and departing, engines must be clearly identifiable so that one can keep track of boxcar positions. In TDM's, engines are frame synchronization characters and are constantly searched for and monitored to insure that the data is distributed properly. Since engines do not carry cargo it is inefficient to use short trains and many engines. Likewise, using too many sync characters or short frames is inefficient in time division multiplexing. Long trains mean that it takes longer to detect when the multiplexer is out of sync, which, in turn, means that a lot of data cargo would be misdelivered in the interim. Most TDM's detect loss of frame registration in about one second, depending on length of frame and aggregate data rate. Under average conditions about 10 characters per channel may be misdirected before the loss of frame sync is detected. This loss of sync delay parameter is usually only of significance in military and secure-data applications. Bit-interleaving units can usually detect the out-of-sync condition faster than character-interleaved units. Additional frame synchronization features are considered in the next chapter.

Multiplexing Efficiency

Since asynchronous terminals operate at all of the rates shown in Table 1-1, a multiplexer should be capable of multiplexing data at any or all of these rates simultaneously; when intermixing data rates and formats, efficiency should be maximized. If the boxcars on the train are all large enough to carry ASCII characters, then they are inefficient carriers of Baudot characters. Ideally, a multiplexer train should utilize a different size boxcar for each type of data it carries. Four different sizes are theoretically required for 5-, 6-, 7-, and 8-level codes but there are few TDM's offering all four.

Even more important in maintaining efficiency in speed intermixing systems is the ability to apportion the boxcars properly among the data shippers. The train runs at a fixed speed determined by the trunk data rate. If one boxcar is assigned to each channel per train and exactly one data character per shipper was waiting to be loaded on each and every train, the efficiency would theoretically be maximized. In practice there must be just a few more boxcars than there are data characters to insure that even if cargo arrives a little faster than expected it can still be handled. Therefore, the normal situation is that all boxcars periodically make a trip either empty or take on a different kind of cargo (control characters — see next chapter). Figure 1-2(a) shows a simple frame that uses none of the sophisticated methods discussed. It has frequent sync characters, equal-size character slots, and uses one slot per channel. Note that a total of eight channels can be accommodated at a trunk rate of 2400 bps.

By adding more boxcars to the train and apportioning them as closely as possible among the data sources in proportion to the amount of cargo they have to ship, efficiency can be markedly improved. Almost all modern multiplexers use the proportional boxcar assignment method. Figure 1-2(b) shows such an efficient multiplexer frame. Note that the 30 character-per-second channel uses three times as many slots as does the 10 character-per-second user. For comparison, an FDM channel spectrum is shown in Figure 1-2(c). In most intermixed situations, the modern TDM is substantially more efficient than its FDM counterpart.

Cost Effective TDM Systems

Once it has been decided to use a multiplexer to save line charges, the question arises as to what multiplexer features yield the most economical system. Some multiplexer characteristics that must be considered are capacity, intermix flexibility, channel interfaces, adaptability, expandability, logic organization, mechanical convenience, field programmability, transparency to data and control, multiplexing delay, frame synchronization stability, and diagnostics.

Awareness of these basic characteristics and how they relate to the requirements of a multichannel network makes it easier to select the best multiplexer and options for a particular application.

SYNC	30	1	2	1	2	3	4	5	SYNC	30	1	2	1	2	3	4	5	SYNC	CHANNEL NUMBER
		15	15	10	10	10	10	10			15	15	10	10	10	10	10		SPEED

|← CHARACTER →| |←——— 1 FRAME ———→|

```
TRUNK CHANNEL CAPACITY AT 2400 BPS      SLOT SIZE
1 CHANNEL @ 30 CHARACTERS PER SECOND      8 BIT    (ASCII)
2 CHANNELS @ 15 CHARACTERS PER SECOND     8 BIT    (IBM)
5 CHANNELS @ 10 CHARACTERS PER SECOND     8 BIT    (ASCII)
```

Figure 1-2(a)/Simple Frame Format of Character-Interleaved Time Division Multiplexer Uses One Slot per Channel per Frame and Constant Slot Size.

SYNC	30	1	2	1	2	3	4	1	2	3	4	30	3	4	5	6	7	8	5	6	7	8	30	1	2	9	10	11	12	9	10	11	SYNC
		15	15	10	10	10	10	10	10	10	10		15	15	10	10	10	10	10	10	10	10		15	15	10	10	10	10	10	10	10	

```
TRUNK CHANNEL CAPACITY — 2400 BPS
1 CHANNEL — 30 CHARACTERS PER SECOND
4 CHANNELS — 15 CHARACTERS PER SECOND
12 CHANNELS — 10 CHARACTERS PER SECOND
11 CHANNELS — 10 CHARACTERS PER SECOND
```

Figure 1-2(b)/Typical Character-Interleaved Multiplexer Frame Using Proportional Slot Assignment and Variable Slot Size to Achieve High Multiplexing Efficiency

```
340        680      1020      1360 Hz
   510        850•   1190    1560    1800    2040 Hz      2520
```

10	10	10	10	10	10	10	15 CPS	15 CPS	30 CPS

```
TRUNK CAPACITY
1 CHANNEL @ 30 CHARACTERS PER SECOND       (ASCII)
2 CHANNELS @ 15 CHARACTERS PER SECOND      (IBM)
7 CHANNELS @ 10 CHARACTERS PER SECOND      (ASCII)
```

Figure 1-2(c)/Typical FDM Format for Unconditioned Voice Grade Line

11

Figure 1-3 shows a typical point-to-point multiplexing system with several types of co-located and remote terminals being multiplexed. Multipoint systems are considered in a later chapter.

To determine the amount of money which can be saved by point-to-point multiplexing, a comparison must be made between the cost of the system without the multiplexer and the cost with it. The expected lifetime of the system is an important consideration in this calculation, since line costs are a recurring monthly expense and the elimination of even one line can result in a substantial saving if a long enough period is involved. The following equation may be used to calculate the savings that obtain:

$$T(N-1)L - M - M_T + M_L - TLS = \text{saving, where}$$

T   = expected lifetime of the system in months

N   = number of channels being multiplexed

L   = monthly line charge between the points being multiplexed

M   = cost of multiplexer

M_T = cost of trunk modems (if any)

M_L = cost of channel modems no longer required

LS = monthly cost of low-speed access lines and modems to multiplexer

Some other factors, both monetary and non-monetary, to add to the above calculation include the cost and availability of maintenance for the multiplexers and their associated modems, the consequences of an outage on the one line between the TDM's or of the TDM's themselves, a possible requirement for a backup line, and the stability of the configuration during its expected lifetime (to avoid early obsolescence of the multiplexer and the cost of frequent reconfiguration).

The Saving Graces of Multiplexing

As shown in Figure 1-3, virtually any data source can be time-multiplexed, including directly connected, dial-up, synchronous, asynchronous, TWX, Telex, and current loop terminals. The multiplexed data trunk may be transmitted via a modem and analog transmission line, via a digital long-distance line, or through a full duplex dial-up connection. Trunk line transmission is usually synchronous but asynchronous transmission is also possible.

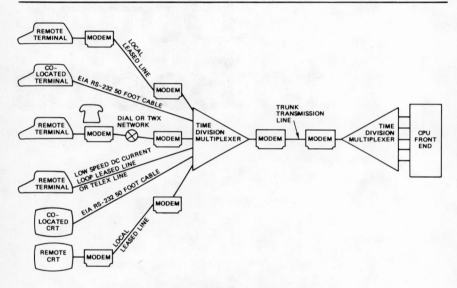

Figure 1-3/Basic Two Point Multiplexing System

2

Down to Basics

BASIC TDM SYSTEMS AND FEATURES

The communications manager should examine his data communications network to see if the savings that can be achieved through multiplexing apply to his network. If the network consists of several terminals at one or more locations communicating with a multiport computer at another location, the system is an excellent candidate for multiplexing. It is not necessary for all the terminals to be in the same room with the multiplexer. Terminals may be connected to nearby multiplexers via the voice, TWX, or Telex dial networks, dedicated voice grade lines, or high voltage current loop telegraph lines. The major consideration in determining whether to multiplex.or not is how much money can be saved. Additional factors, such as grade of service, availability of the system, reliability, and ease of maintenance of the resulting system, should also be taken into account. Once a decision to multiplex is made, a decision as to what type of multiplexer and what features it requires must be made. The following paragraphs are a guide to making this an informed decision.

Mechanical Features
The mechanical design philosophy used in building a time-division multiplexer is much more significant to the user than is the case with, say, a modem, a product which comes quite close to being the legendary black box. A poor mechanical construction technique can cost the user a significant amount of money or inconvenience when even minor reconfiguration or re-installation is required.

All TDM's have common logic, channel interface, and power supply sections. Virtually all multiplexers consist of one or more racks into which are plugged the common logic, the channel interface cards, and sometimes the power supply. Such plug-in card-cage construction makes it easy to effect repairs by means of card exchange. Where multiplexers differ mechanically is in the method used to interface low-speed channels to the central logic. Some TDM's use one interface card per channel. The virtues of this procedure are that, when a card is extracted for repair, only one channel is interrupted and, in mixed interface systems, no odd number of channels need ever be left unused. TDM's with 2, 4, and even 24 channels per card are available and have the advantage of low cost and compactness. Multiple channel cards usually have fewer per-channel diagnostics and any option or strappings must apply to all the channels on the card. Thus, a single two-channel card could not be used to service both an asynchronous channel and a synchronous channel.

Cable connectors are an important part of the cost of a multiplexer. These connectors may be mounted on the channel cards themselves or on the back plane of the card assembly. The advantage of the former method is that one need only pay for those connectors he plans to use, and that different types of channel cards can have different types of connectors, saving the cost of cable adapters. This apparent price advantage is not always realized in practice, since several of the lowest-cost, small-system multiplexers mount the channel cable connectors on the back plane and yet are extremely price competitive. If the connectors are mounted on the cards, the cable must be removed when the channel card is repaired, an inconvenience which may be crucial in some environments. If the connector is at the rear of the card, then slack must be left to make it possible to remove the card from the front and then release the cable. In this way, rear access is not essential when making repairs. In at least one TDM the cable connectors are on the front of the channel cards. While such placement is convenient for installing or moving cables between channels, it is often difficult to get clearance for such bulky cables in the front of standard cabinets and the cable wires hide diagnostic controls and lamps.

Multiplexing Capacity

Three factors determine how many channels a given multiplexer can multiplex. The first is the mechanical capacity of the system — how many channel cards can be used with one set of central logic? Basic TDM units are available in such sizes as 4, 9, 12, 16, 20, and 24 channels. These units may then be expanded, usually by adding more channel-card cages. The limit in such units is the channel capacity of the central logic and the power supply capacity. In some cases, expansion is achieved by interconnecting complete multiplexers, each with its own common logic and power supply. The former approach is less costly for large systems but requires a large initial investment even when starting small. The latter method becomes unreliable, bulky, and expensive very quickly as the number of channels grows. For example, a 48-channel system would require four complete TDM units if constructed from 12-channel basic units and would therefore be four times as likely to fail as a 48-channel multiplexer using one set of common logic and four expansion rack assemblies.

The second limitation on multiplexing is the data rate at which the aggregate data stream is clocked — a figure usually determined by the modem or facility used, typically on the order of 2400, 4800, 7200, or 9600 bits per second. A multiplexer running at 4800 bps can multiplex twice as many characters per second as one running at 2400 bps.

The third factor in determining multiplexing capacity has to do with the flexibility of the multiplexer logic in frame establishment. Can slots be assigned in exact proportion to the character rates of the data sources? Must start and stop bits multiplexed? Can smaller aggregate stream characters be used for Baudot or IBM coded data sources? How much overhead is used for frame synchronization characters? The following formula may be used to determine quite closely how many channels of asynchronous mixed-speed data can be multiplexed in a typical multiplexer:

$$(A - \Sigma_i S_i)\ .97 \geqslant N_1 C_1 L_1 + N_2 C_2 L_2 + N_3 C_3 L_3 + \ldots N_i C_i L_i$$

where A = aggregate stream data rate in bits per second

S_i = rate in bits per second of any synchronous data being multiplexed

N_i = number of channels being multiplexed at each speed and code

C_i = rounded-up character rates of the data sources. If C_1 is the highest character rate in the system, then $C_2, C_3, \ldots$ C_i must be rounded up to the nearest whole fraction of C_1, i.e., 1/1, 1/2, 1/3, 1/4, 1/5, etc.

L_2 = number of bits per character multiplexed on the aggregate line for a particular C_i. May be 6, 7, 8, or 9, depending on the sophistication of the particular multiplexer.

The above equation gives good results for most of the multiplexers on the market. It can be made exact for a particular multiplexer by determining the slot size (L) and the intermix fractions (how much the slower channel rates must be rounded up to fit the frame) for the particular TDM being considered. In an older multiplexer without intermix capability, all the C_i's and L_i's are equal to the highest C_i or L_i in the system and are all the same. For example, if A = 2400 bps and we wish to know how many 110 baud channels can be multiplexed with four 300 baud channels in a multiplexer with a fixed high-speed slot of 9 bits per character, no intermix capability, and no synchronous data being multiplexed, then, from the formula:

$$(2400-0) \ .97 = 4 \times 30 \times 9 + N_2 \times 30 \times 9$$

$$N_2 = 4.6 = 4 \text{ channels}$$

Now let us repeat the calculation for a modern multiplexer with efficient speed intermix capability. In this case we assume that a mixed 8- and 9-bit slot size is possible and $C_2 = 10$ (from Table 1-1)

$$(2400-0) \ .97 = 4 \times 30 \times 9 + N_2 \times 10 \times 8$$

$$N_2 = 15.6 = 15 \text{ channels}$$

The ratio of C_1 to C_2 in this case is 1/3, a whole number fraction, so no rounding up is required.

As a last example, let us check the frame shown in Figure 1-2(b). In that example:

A = 2400 bps
S = 0

$C_1 = 30$	$N_1 = 1$	$L_1 = 8$
$C_2 = 15$	$N_2 = 4$	$L_2 = 7$
$C_3 = 10$	$N_3 = 12$	$L_3 = 8$
$C_4 = 10$	$N_4 = 11$	$L_4 = 6$

$$2400 \times .97 \geqslant 1 \times 30 \times 8 + 4 \times 15 \times 7 + 10 \times 12 \times 8 + 10 \times 11 \times 6$$

$$2328 \geqslant 240 + 420 + 960 + 660$$

$$2328 \geqslant 2280$$

Since the equation is true, it is possible for a multiplexer to multiplex this combination of channels at 2400 bps if it has a variable slot size, uses an 8-bit slot for ASCII data and can handle speed ratios of 1/2 and 1/3.

Frame Geometry

In order to establish efficient multiplexing frames, it is necessary to fix a method of frame programming. The bits or characters available must be divided up and assigned to the low-speed channels so that no channel has too few slots, which would cause a loss of data, or too many, which would mean a loss of efficiency. There are as many types of multiplexer frames as there are multiplexer manufacturers; this diversity — plus the variations in frame sync characters — is why TDM's of different manufacturers cannot talk to each other. Quite often even different models of TDM's from the same manufacturer are not compatible. There are certain universal principles, however, which are common to all TDM's.

19

First, an overall frame length is established. The length of this frame usually is set so that the frame repetition rate is just slightly faster than the character rate of the slowest channel to be multiplexed. Sync characters mark the beginning of each frame. It is possible to skip sync characters between some frames but the basic concept is not altered. The frame is then divided into timeslots; sometimes the timeslots are subdivided into character slots. Each manufacturer has different names for these subdivisions (e.g., sections, segments, frame units, bytes, timewidths, fractions), but the principle is the same. Each channel to be multiplexed is assigned to as many slots in the frame (boxcars) as it requires.

The assignment process usually must be done in such a manner that buffering requirements are minimized. For example, in Figure 1-2(b) the 30-character-per-second channel is assigned three slots, placed at even intervals, in every frame. If they were placed adjacent to each other, it would be necessary to accumulate and store up to four characters for that channel instead of two — the additional storage would increase the peak multiplexing delay and the logic cost.

Frame Programming

Once an efficient frame is established on paper, it is necessary to program the multiplexer by setting the frame length and, if applicable, the trunk modem data rate, and by assigning each channel to the proper slot or slots (analogous to establishing the length of the train, speed of the train, and order of the boxcars).

Multiplexer programming varies with the manufacturer and is done with straps, plugs, cable connectors, wire wrapping on the back plane, and read-only memories. Ease of programming is an extremely important property of a multiplexer. Programming methods that require special parts from the factory or rewiring of logic nests can be both expensive and quite irritating if used in systems where reconfiguration must be done frequently. TDM's that can be reprogrammed in the field by the user are the most desirable, but if special tools or

20

soldering are required, they may not be truly field programmable by semi-skilled computer-room technicians. It is also
desirable to be able to change the speed or code of one or
two channels without affecting other channels that are on-
line or having to power down the TDM.

When non-volatile ROM's are used as repositories of the
frame geometry, it is possible to use several of them, each
with a different frame program, and to switch manually or
remotely from one program to another as desired. But each
time the TDM is reconfigured, a new ROM must be ordered
from the manufacturer. Read-write volatile memory has also
been used to program multiplexers, but a logic glitch, power
shutdown, or failure in such systems requires a reloading of
the program. An advantage of the alterable frame memory
is that a computer can electronically reprogram the multiplexer system.

Logic Organization and Redundancy

There are two possible approaches to multiplexer design. In
the first, almost all buffering and processing is done in common logic; therefore, the channel cards can be simpler and
less expensive. In the second approach, each channel card has
its own character buffers, frame program counters, and diagnostics; thus, the central logic can be simple and inexpensive.
The latter technique has the advantage of decreasing the probability that a logic failure would cause all lines to go down at
once. It also makes spare cards or a redundant common logic
system less costly. However, such a design approach requires
extremely complex channel cards and increases the number
of logic devices in a system of even moderate size, thereby
significantly increasing the cost, dimensions, and power con-
sumption of the unit. The fact that a very large, and therefore vulnerable, power supply becomes necessary in the channel-card logic approach counteracts its advantages. Furthermore, if only the amount of down time per channel is considered, the system that would have the highest reliability and
least amount of down time is the system with the fewest

logic elements per channel (per-channel logic plus common logic divided by the number of channels multiplexed) and the least stressed power supply.

Doing as much as possible in common logic usually results in a relatively inexpensive channel card; therefore, this approach is most economical for large systems. It does mean, however, that while single channel failures are rare, common logic failures are more probable. In this type of system, redundant central logic is a good investment if complete system failure cannot be tolerated. In the first approach, redundant common logic buys little in a system where 95% of the hardware is on the channel cards.

Where redundant central logic is offered, the question arises as to how the central logic can monitor its own failures and switch over. No such system is infallible, but the switchover is backed up by remote and local manual controls. Various signals, such as loss of frame sync, key timing pulses, and the continuous pseudo-multiplexing and demultiplexing of a test character, can all be used to detect a central logic failure and initiate automatic switchover.

Frame Synchronization Criteria

Barring a logic failure, the only way a multiplexing system can lose frame synchronization is if the modem or device that is clocking the TDM skips a cycle with respect to the data. With good modems, such an event is extremely rare, since the circuits used in such equipment can maintain bit and clock integrity for many seconds, even if the transmission line is cut. A multiplexer should not go through frequent re-sync cycles simply because an occasional sync bit is received in error due to line noise.

A time division multiplexer is, therefore, protected against going into constant resync cycles by logic which looks at many characters or bits over a period of time before deciding that the system is truly out of sync. Most multiplexers have sync systems whose send and receive directions are independent. Thus a remote multiplexer can search for sync on its receive side while still outputting a normal data stream on its send side. This ability makes it possible for the out-of-sync TDM to send a signal to the other mux telling it that it is out of sync. Out-of-sync alarm features are considered in a later chapter.

Overspeed Compensation

Multiplexers reclock asynchronous data when they demultiplex it. It is possible that the demultiplexer clock is marginally slower than the clock used to generate the data at its source or that the source is running fast and outputting slightly more characters per second than the demultiplexer is expecting. In the train analogy, this situation means that more cargo is arriving than can be removed from the unloading platform. When the platform is full, the next boxcar cannot be unloaded and its cargo is destroyed. To prevent these losses, there are several solutions possible. One is to provide forklifts and extra unloading equipment so that offloading can proceed fast enough that cargo never accumulates; a disadvantage is that cargo may be delivered slightly faster than it is really wanted. In electronic terms, the speed-up is accomplished by increasing the data rate clock enough to insure that all data can be demultiplexed and outputted as fast as it is received. Alternatively, just the rest bit between characters can be shortened to achieve the same effect. However, some terminals are sensitive to such a speed-up of the data or abbreviation of rest bits.

A better, more sophisticated, speed compensation method is to note when the loading platform is filling up with cargo, and then to accelerate the shipping operation for just as long as it takes to empty the platform. This dynamic method has the advantage of not requiring a continuous amount of fixed speed-up and is particularly useful where multiplexers are used in tandem. Where TDM's are used in series over many shorter links, each succeeding multiplexer must cope with any speed-up in the multiplexer ahead of it by speeding up the demultiplexed data still more. The dynamic speed compensation method reduces the magnitude of any speed-up effect and permits any number of such TDM's to be used in tandem.

A third method (common in other communications equipment but uncommon in multiplexers) is to send a message to the shipper whenever the loading platform is full, requesting a short halt to shipments until the backlog is cleared. This method introduces no distortion in data or rest bits and causes no cumulative speed-up in tandem multiplexer links.

Data Transparency

Virtually all time division multiplexers pass all the characters in the code set used by the data source they are multiplexing. However, in multiplexers that do not multiplex start and stop bits, some means must be found to distinguish between an all-space character and a spacing line, and between an all-marks character and a marking line. Or, in other words, the demultiplexer must be told when not to insert rest bits on a spacing line and when not to put start bits on a marking line. The messages that transmit this type of information are usually called control bits or characters and multiplexers usually transmit many other kinds of control and diagnostic information. Since efficiency requires that control information for a given channel be sent in the same slot as data, the trick is to transmit such control data without confusing it with data or interfering with data transmission. Control characters are often distinguished by adding a bit to each character that indicates whether the character is data or control. Control characters are sent whenever no data is ready to be sent. This method is effective but decreases efficiency by 10 to 20%, depending on the character length. A more efficient method can be used with codes that have a parity bit by making normal parity, data and reverse parity, control. Trouble can arise under noisy line conditions, since data characters may be distorted to look like control characters and thus be deleted, or control characters may become data characters and be outputted. However, experience in thousands of systems has shown that these effects are rare and no more disruptive than the errors that occur on unmultiplexed transmission lines.

Adaptive Channel Multiplexers

An option common in the newer multiplexers permits a variety of terminals operating at different rates and codes to access a multiplexer via the dial network. The same phone number is dialed by all users of the system and the callers are assigned by the telephone equipment to whichever multiplexer channels are free. Since there is no way to determine which terminal will be operating with which channel card, it is impossible to program the channels in advance. The multiplexer must automatically adapt to each caller as the calls are answered. Computer front ends have the same problem when operating in dial-up systems but are now available with adaptive features so that they are fully compatible with an adaptive multiplexer.

There are several methods used to detect the speed of the incoming data. In most cases, a special predetermined first character must be sent by the terminal. This character is detected at some idle speed and decoded to determine the speed of the terminal that sent it. The multiplexer can then shift from the idle speed to the terminal speed. This character or another control character can then be sent to the remote multiplexer to tell it what the speed of the channel is. Once the multiplexers have adapted, a character can be sent by the terminal or by the multiplexer to cause the computer front end to adapt. Between calls the multiplexers are reset to the idle speed, based on the lowering of a control signal such as "Carrier Detect" (see Chapter 4).

Another adaptive method is to measure the bit period of the received data to determine its speed, but this method is only reliable if the speeds expected are substantially different and the first character mark-space pattern of faster terminals is carefully chosen not to mimic legitimate slower-speed data.

A disadvantage of both these types of adaptive multiplexers is that the terminal sign-on protocol for dialing via the TDM is not usually the same as it is for terminals calling a computer directly. This discrepancy can cause operator confusion in circumstances where a terminal normally makes calls to more than one computer, some via multiplexers and some not. A more significant disadvantage lies in the fact that the presently available multiplexers do not reprogram the frame slots adaptively. Therefore all adaptive speed channels in the mux must be so programmed that enough high-speed line slots are available to service the fastest terminal expected to call in. The result is an average inefficiency that reduces the maximum number of channels that can be multiplexed.

As an example, if forty terminals in a city can dial a local multiplexer and the terminals are mixed 10-, 15-, and 30-characters per second, all the channel cards must be programmed for frame slots of 30 cps. Thus, if a 2400 bps trunk is assumed, only 9 channels can be multiplexed at once, even though the 9 channels might be 10 cps and in theory 29 channels could be handled at this rate. Theoretically, adaptive framing is possible but, at present, it appears to be impractical to implement in hard-wired multiplexers. For these reasons, adaptive system users seldom attempt to mix 1200 baud and 110 baud terminals adaptively.

Channel Card Types
A multiplexer, if it is to be truly universal, must interface to as wide a variety of data sources as possible. The most common data interface is the one defined in EIA RS-232. A

channel card is needed to connect to terminals and modems using this interface (see Chapter 11 for details on the EIA interface).

Another interface is the high voltage current loop interface commonly used by Baudot coded 50 and 75 baud terminals. Several 2-wire, 4-wire, polar, or neutral current loop interfaces are possible, so a current loop channel card, to be flexible, must have many strap options.

Channel cards may also be provided with built-in 103 or 202 equivalent modems for direct connection to low-speed leased or dial-up lines. Most multiplexers also use different channel card types for asynchronous and synchronous data. Data interfaces compatible with the 303 modem and a bi-polar interface compatible with the CSU (Channel Service Unit) of the DDS network are needed in some wideband systems. Mil Standard and Overseas specifications (CCITT) may require still more varieties of channel card.

Since there is no uniformity in the type of connectors all the various channel card types require, adapter cables are often necessary. The majority of multiplexers use the female 25-pin EIA RS-232 specified connector, so an adapter with a male connector at one end and spade lugs, barrier strip terminals, or some other connector at the opposite end is normally required for all non-RS-232 channels. Those TDM's that can mount the connectors directly on the channel cards do not require such adapters, but such multiplexers are rare.

The Reinstitution of Slavery

SYNCHRONOUS DATA MULTIPLEXING

Synchronous Data and Synchronous Data Clocking

Synchronous data is data whose rate and transition time are under the direct or indirect control of a master clock. The master clock is usually the fastest clock in a system. Any slower synchronous data clocks are derived from it, either by digital division or other digital logic technique. All the clocks derived from the master clock are referred to as slave clocks in this and subsequent chapters. Slave clocks need not be synchronized continuously to the master clock. In certain controlled circumstances they may be allowed to drift faster or slower for short periods, provided that over a known period of time the number of slave-clock cycles is still precisely related to the master clock.

Since the slave clocks are derived digitally from the master clock, there are certain fundamental limitations imposed by the laws of electronics. They require that all slave-clock rates be expressed as whole-number fractions of the master clock. Therefore, a slave clock can be 1/2, 1/3, 1/4, 2/3, 5/9, etc., of the master clock, but cannot be $1/\pi$ or $1/e$. For practical reasons, the denominator of such fractions is limited (256 or usually even less). It is also possible to multiply a master clock to yield a higher slave clock, should one be needed. Again, multiplication logic requires that integer fraction relationships be maintained. In most of the systems being discussed, the master clock originates in the modem and the slave clocks are generated in the multiplexer or modem front end.

There is a distinct difference between the clock accuracy requirements for driving synchronous modems and driving synchronous terminals. Synchronous modems are designed to operate at precisely defined data rates with tolerances on the order of .01% to .001%. Even if clocked by an external clock, this accuracy must be maintained, lest the modem error rate

increase or the modem go into constant retrain cycles (if
adaptively equalized). Most voiceband modems operate at
1200, 1800, 2000, 2400, 3600, 4800, 7200, or 9600 bps.
Therefore, if multiplexers are to interface to modems on
either the aggregate or the low-speed side, they must operate
precisely at one of these rates. Wideband synchronous data
rates include, historically, 19.2, 40.8, 50, and 230.4 kbps,
although 56 and 230.4 kbps are the only domestic wideband
services now currently available. The new DDS network offers 2.4, 4.8, 9.6, and 56 kbps service; overseas, 16, 32, and
64 kbps facilities are available in some countries. However,
the fact remains that synchronous transmission facilities,
either through modems or through the new digital networks,
are provided at fixed, invariable rates, and the multiplexer
user and designer must live with this fact.

By contrast, synchronous terminals and computer ports are
essentially passive devices and, with only rare exceptions, are
quite tolerant of clock frequency variations. For instance, a
CRT terminal or its computer port designed to operate at
2400 bps can usually be clocked at 2300 or 1800 bps without ill effect. It is even possible to delete or skip entire clock
cycles without the terminal or computer being aware of the
hesitation. Some time division multiplexers of asynchronous
data are equivalent to synchronous terminals and may be
clocked at arbitrary frequencies. However, not all TDM's are
alike in this regard. Some adapt themselves to any aggregate
bit rate automatically, while others must be strapped to operate at a particular aggregate rate. Often the strapping is required because an internal oscillator is being synchronized to
the external clock, and such oscillators need to be set to a
nominal value to track properly.

Synchronous Multiplexer Clocking Arrangements

Knowing why and when particular modems in a given system
must be externally clocked — and which of these must be

clocked by their own receive clocks — is one of the most difficult concepts in multiplexing theory to master.

Figure 3-1 illustrates a simplified synchronous terminal-to-computer multiplexer system. Data, control signals, and the

FOR SIMPLICITY ONLY THE CLOCK LEADS
OF A SINGLE CHANNEL ARE SHOWN

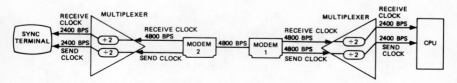

Figure 3-1/The simplest of the synchronous multiplexing configurations requires send and receive clock dividers.

other channels being multiplexed have been omitted for simplicity. Modem 1 generates a 4800 bps send data clock. Each cycle of this clock asks for a bit from the multiplexer. The multiplexer in its turn asks the computer for a bit every other clock cycle. The multiplexer generates the 2400 bps clock in this example by dividing the modem 4800 bps clock by 2. The bit of data from the CPU is multiplexed, modulated, and sent over the line to the remote modem, where a 4800 bps receive clock is recovered by the modem from the received data stream. This receive clock is identical in average frequency to the send clock oscillator in the modem at the computer (although variable delay or Doppler shift on the line may cause short-term drift from time to time). This receive clock is then divided by two to produce the 2400 bps clock needed to drive the receive side of the CRT terminal. In the reverse direction, the master clock is at the CRT and the data-derived clock is at the computer.

In reality, many multiplexers cannot operate this way because they have only one divider circuit for both the send and receive clocks. This measure is more than just one for economy since, as will be shown, when synchronous modems

31

are multiplexed, it is impossible to use two dividers. Also, in more sophisticated systems, where synchronous data rates are often fairly complex fractions of the trunk data rate, the burden of double clock programming for every synchronous channel becomes too heavy. Therefore, the clocking arrangement of Figure 3-2 is common with only one synchronous clock divider to divide the modem clock. At the slave end, the modem receive clock is cross-connected to the multiplexer send clock input, serving as both receive and send clock. Of course, the modem must be strapped for external clock and the receive clock signal looped to drive it. The TDM and the modem then are synchronized in the send direction. These cross connections are made either in special cables or by straps in the multiplexer.

FOR SIMPLICITY ONLY THE CLOCK LEADS AND A
SINGLE LOW SPEED CHANNEL ARE SHOWN

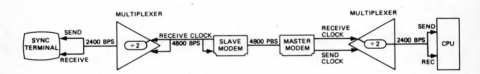

Figure 3-2/If only one clock divider is used in the multiplexers, the remote modem must be externally clocked by its own receive data clock.

Figure 3-3 illustrates the synchronous clocking required when a pair of synchronous modems is interposed between the CRT terminal and the multiplexer. Starting at the master modem location (1), data is extracted from the computer by a 2400 bps clock. This clock is derived directly from the master modem 4800 bps clock by the divide-by-two circuit. The computer data is then multiplexed, modulated, transmitted to the remote modem, and demodulated. The data is clocked into

the multiplexer by modem 2's receive clock at 4800 bps, demultiplexed, and clocked into modem 3 by a 2400 bps send
clock derived from the 4800 bps receive clock for transmission to the remote CRT. At the end of the 2400 bps line, the
data is fed into the terminal under the control of the 2400
bps clock recovered by the modem from the data stream.
Presently, therefore, all the clocks in the data path, from the
computer to the terminal, are synchronized, provided that
the third modem is externally clocked. But let us see what
happens when data goes from the terminal to the computer.
If modem 4 were clocked by its own internal 2400 bps send
data oscillator, it would take data from the terminal at that

FOR SIMPLICITY ONLY THE CLOCK LEADS AND A
SINGLE LOW SPEED CHANNEL ARE SHOWN

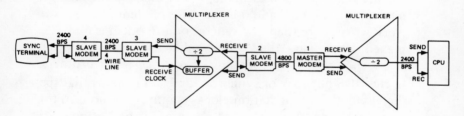

*Figure 3-3/The modems, in tail circuits between multiplexers
and synchronous terminals, must be slaved.*

clock rate, modulate and then transmit it to modem 3. Modem 3 would demodulate it, recover clock, and deliver the
data to the multiplexer for multiplexing. The multiplexer
trunk line, however, is clocked by the modem 2 receive clock
and, after division by two, the internal multiplexer 2400 bps
clock is not precisely equal to the 2400 bps receive data clock
of modem 3. Either too many or too few bits of data are
multiplexed. Even if substantial amounts of buffering are
provided, the buffer eventually under- or over-flows, and errors occur. Therefore, modem 4 cannot be allowed to have a

free-running send clock. The solution is to loop the receive data clock as shown. Now the data being multiplexed is synchronized with the data being demultiplexed at this point in the system. For this to be true, in turn, requires that the send and receive clocks of modem 2 be identical, which is indeed the case. As shown, modem 2 is wired as a slave modem timed by its own receive clock, driving both send and receive sides of the multiplexer. Since modem 2 is looped, the send and receive clocks at modem 1 are identical and the entire system is synchronized. Finally, because all send and receive clock pairs must be synchronized in these systems, separate send and receive clock dividers are superfluous, and the general rule that only one master clock per system is allowed has few exceptions.

An alternative clocking scheme, where the receive clock of modem 3 is doubled and used to drive modem 2, does not work when more than one synchronous modem is multiplexed. In any case, the slower modem oscillators are often not accurate or stable enough to drive their faster brothers.

In the DDS network or synchronous TDM systems that span the globe, the use of station clocks is quite common. In this case, TDM's and modems both operate off the station clock at each location. It is assumed that the station clocks are of such stability and accuracy that no bits are lost and synchronous modems can function without error. Although modem clocks are shown in the systems below, the configurations illustrated are easily adapted to station clock operation or operation without modems via the DDS network.

Split Stream Modems

An ingenious and reliable synchronous multiplexing technique is a serendipitous result of the development of 4800, 7200, and 9600 bps modems. A 9600 bps modem, for example, takes bits four at a time and, depending on the value of the four bits, encodes them as one of sixteen possible phase and/or amplitude values of a carrier. Thus, a 9600 bps modem encoding bits four at a time is actually signalling at a rate of 2400 baud. On each cycle of a 2400 Hz clock, therefore, four bits of data can be accepted from four terminals, encoded, modulated, demodulated, decoded, and outputted in parallel, on four corresponding output lines clocked by a 2400 bps clock recovered from the received data stream. At 7200 bps, bits are taken three at a time, and at 4800, two at a time. Therefore, three 2400 bps terminals can be multiplexed by a 7200 bps modem, and two by a 4800 bps modem. For further flexibility, 4800 bps can be multiplexed with 2400 bps at 7200 bps by feeding two out of each three bits to the same modem port. Similarly, any combination of 2400, 4800, or 7200 bps channels that add up to 9600 can be handled.

Note that this form of synchronous data multiplexing is self-framing and therefore 100% efficient. All other synchronous data multiplexers must provide for either synchronization bits or stuffing characters, or must monitor the data stream to ensure channel synchronization. The split-stream modem, however, maintains positive channel synchronization without sync bits on random data because the frame synchronization is inherent in the encoding and decoding process. For example, if the four bits being multiplexed at 9600 bps are 1 0 0 1 for channels 1, 2, 3, and 4, respectively, and if such a bit pattern is represented by a phase shift of +90° and 3/4 amplitude, then when that phase shift and amplitude are detected by the demodulator, it checks its memory and sees that 90° and 3/4 amplitude mean that the bits 1 0 0 1 should be put on the lines to channels 1, 2, 3, and 4 in that exact order.

Figures 3-4 and 3-5 show several of the most common applications for split-stream modems. They can be used in point-to-point and multipoint polling systems, and can multiplex multiplexers, terminals, and computers. Some of the early split stream modems were limited, particularly in polling applications, because they could not transmit control signals on a per-channel basis, and could not buffer or re-time data received from other modems. However, the latest crop of split-stream modems has buffers large enough to buffer half-duplex data as described below, and function in Doppler shift environments. They also provide per-channel independent RTS-CTS delays and actually transmit the carrier detect signals from modems being multiplexed (by sending a special repetitive code when modem carrier is not present and data is therefore not being transmitted). Also, they may be externally clocked by one of the channels being multiplexed, a necessary

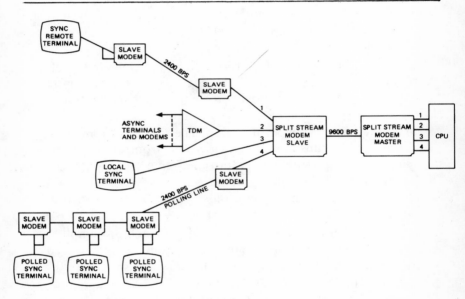

Figure 3-4/Four common applications of split-stream modems.

feature when the split-stream modem itself is being multiplexed, as in Figure 3-5(c). The only serious disadvantage of the split-stream modems is their relative inflexibility — since they are pretty much limited to a maximum of four channels at fractional rates of 1/4, 1/3, 1/2, 2/3, and 3/4. They can only be used at voiceband rates, they cannot handle asynchronous data (except in the grossly inefficient manner of sampling a teletype channel at a 2400 bps rate), and are of no use if DDS facilities are used.

Combining Split-Stream Modems and Asynchronous TDM's

In Figure 3-5 some typical systems are assembled which can be implemented using split-stream modems, single-stream modems, and asynchronous time division multiplexers. The systems are illustrative, and other synchronous data rates and arrangements are equally possible. Figure 3-5 also illustrates how a synchronous modem with an independent reverse channel can be used as a simple multiplexer, multiplexing one CRT terminal at 2400 bps, and one asynchronous teletype at 10 or 15 characters per second.

Bit-Interleaving Synchronous Data Channel Adapters

One of the simplest ways to add the multiplexing of synchronous data to a standard asynchronous TDM is to alternate part of the data from a synchronous terminal with part from a multiplexer trunk stream to form a new trunk data stream. Several early asynchronous TDM's offered such adapters, and Figure 3-6 shows the basic elements of such an accessory. The sync channel adapter consisted primarily of a clock divider, bit switcher, and interface circuitry. Control signals, if any, were multiplexed on a spare channel of the asynchronous TDM. Such adapters were essentially independent of the main multiplexer, except for an out-of-frame sync input to tell the bit switcher when it was feeding the wrong alternate to the TDM.

This approach to sync data multiplexing, while low in cost, is quite primitive and suffers from the disadvantage that only a few channels at one-half, one-third, or one-quarter of the

Figure 3-5/Typical Multiplexing Systems Using Split-Stream Modems

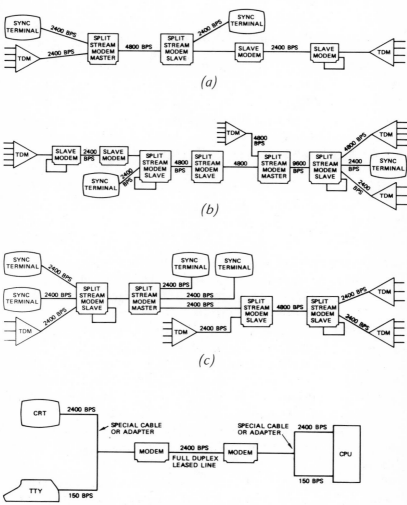

(a)

(b)

(c)

(d)/A modem with an independent full-duplex reverse channel feature may be used as a simple multiplexer.

trunk rate can be handled before the problem of frame synchronization becomes too complex. In addition, the aggregate bit-interleaved format makes software demultiplexing impractical.

Synchronous Data Channel Cards for Asynchronous TDM's

There is an alternate approach to simple bit-interleaving to provide a synchronous multiplexer — allow the data to be processed by the asynchronous TDM common logic system by forming the synchronous data into characters and multiplexing them in essentially the same manner that asynchronous characters are multiplexed. In the case of synchronous data characters, however, no start, stop, or parity bits need be stripped or reinserted, and no idle bits or characters may be added or deleted between synchronous data characters on output.

The advantage of this character-interleaved approach is that the central logic of the multiplexer (sync recovery, formatting, buffering, etc.) is shared by the synchronous channels,

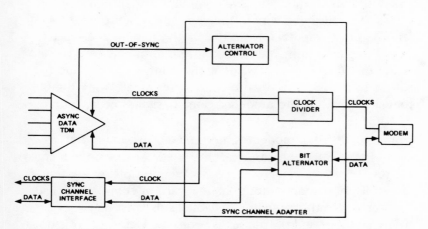

Figure 3-6/Typical Synchronous Data Interleaving Adapter for Use with Asynchronous TDM's

making the channel cards simpler than they would be otherwise. Many of the diagnostics (such as redundant central logic, loopback features, and central logic tests) apply equally to the synchronous and the asynchronous channels. In addition, it is not necessary to limit the number or data rates of the synchronous channels multiplexed, provided that the frame format program system is flexible enough to allow dividing the trunk bits among the channels in fractions exactly proportional to their rates, as discussed earlier.

The following is an example of the type of synchronous data multiplexing flexibility required in some systems; it is desired to multiplex a 2000 bps channel on a 4800 bps trunk. If this is to be done synchronously, exactly five-twelfths of the bits available must be assigned to the 2000 baud channel and a 2000 bps clock synchronized to 4800 bps must also be generated. Neither the split-stream modem nor the simple bit-interleaving technique is adequate to do this.

Synchronous Interface to the Multiplexer

There are four common synchronous channel interfaces between terminals, modems, and computer ports. Figure 3-7(a) shows the leads between multiplexers and synchronous data terminals or computers. Note that both the send and receive clocks originate in the multiplexer. The terminals are assumed to be full duplex, to require no active control signals, and to adhere to RS-232 specifications. Both terminals think that they are connected to modems. Control signals need not be multiplexed.

In Figure 3-7(b), a modem is multiplexed to a computer, assuming that full duplex operation is used. At the modem end, the receive data clock is an input to the multiplexer and, unless a different synchronous channel card or connector is used to interface to the modem, the cable leads must be twisted to match input and output leads properly. Here also, it is not necessary to transmit control signals between the multiplexers. In Figure 3-8(a), a terminal is multiplexed to a computer, but

40

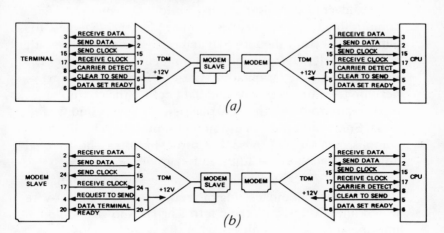

*PIN NUMBERS USED AT THE MULTIPLEXER END OF THE CABLES
SHOWN WILL VARY WITH THE MANUFACTURER SINCE NO
STANDARD HAS BEEN AGREED TO AT PRESENT

Figure 3-7/Full-Duplex Synchronous Channel Interface to
Terminal and Modem

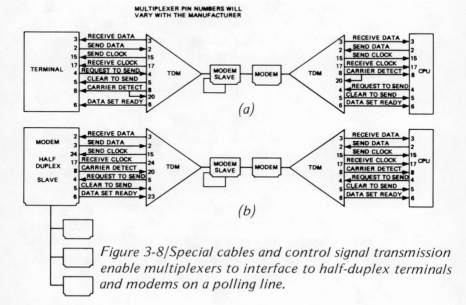

MULTIPLEXER PIN NUMBERS WILL
VARY WITH THE MANUFACTURER

Figure 3-8/Special cables and control signal transmission
enable multiplexers to interface to half-duplex terminals
and modems on a polling line.

the computer is polling the terminal and expects to see "Carrier Detect" come on in response to its poll. Since there is no modem in this system, the multiplexer must fool the computer and simulate this modem function. One method of accomplishing this "trickery" is to multiplex the "Request to Send" signal from the terminal and output it at the computer end as "Carrier Detect" and then loop back this "Carrier Detect" signal to the terminal as "Clear to Send." In this manner, the terminal does not send data before the computer is made ready for it by the "Carrier Detect" signal, and vice versa. Some multiplexers use simple time delay circuits to accomplish the same purpose, but throughput may be affected unless the delay can be adjusted to a minimum value.

In Figure 3-8(b), the computer is polling several terminals via a multiplexer and a string of remote modems on a 4-wire leased line. In this case, the control signals shown should be multiplexed and transmitted, as in the asynchronous data channel case.

Control signals or reverse channel information may be transmitted either separately, via an asynchronous channel, or in band, encoded as special characters in the synchronous data frame slot whenever synchronous data is not being transmitted. This action is possible since whenever a control signal, such as "Carrier Detect" or "Data Set Ready," is off, there can be no data to transmit and the channel is always open for the sending of control signal information.

Dial-Up Synchronous Channel Multiplexing

Sometimes the synchronous channels are connected to the multiplexer via the dial network, as shown in Figure 3-9. Since a dial connection is 2-wire half-duplex, and much of the time there is no receive data to recover clock from, it is impossible to use the receive clock as a send clock at the terminal end of the line. The remote modem must therefore operate as a master, using its own internal oscillator. Since the multiplexer clock and the receive data clock are not synchronized, the data must be buffered at the multiplexer interface. If the oscillators are reasonably accurate and the buffer is large enough, substantial blocks of data can be transferred before buffer overflow or underflow occurs. For example, a ±4 bit buffer, on a 2000 bps channel with a frequency difference between the modem and multiplexer clocks of .02%, can process a block of 2500 characters before an error occurs. This figure is larger than that for the typical data blocks used in bi-sync format systems. The buffer is reset, by Carrier Detect, to its midpoint each time the line turns around. Buffers provided in split-stream modems serve a similar function and, likewise, permit the multiplexing of accurate 2-wire synchronous modems. In dial-up channel multiplexing, true control signal transmission is mandatory and, as shown in Figure 3-9, "Ring Indicator" and "Data Terminal Ready" should be transmitted in addition to "Carrier Detect," "Request to Send," and "Clear to Send."

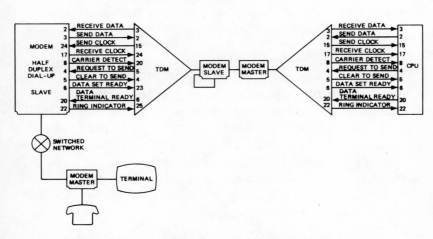

Figure 3-9/Interface Leads Between a Multiplexer and a Dial-Up Synchronous Modem

Isochronous Data Multiplexing

For the purposes of this book, isochronous data is data that is neither synchronous nor formatted in one of the standard asynchronous data formats. Several examples of such data follow, and if not all are truly isochronous (equal bit periods), I hope the reader overlooks the license, since a better word for such data is not available.

A source of synchronous data that is exclusively clocked by its own internal clock, rather than by a modem or a multiplexer, is, by our definition here, isochronous. A synchronous data stream unaccompanied by a receive data clock is also isochronous, as far as most multiplexers or modems are concerned. Some common sources of isochronous data are encryption devices, 2-wire dial-up synchronous terminals, satellite links, or multiplexers whose trunk lines cannot be synchronized conveniently to a master clock.

An example of non-standard asynchronous data that can be regarded as isochronous is a stream of data characters, each headed by a start bit and followed by 35 data bits with one or more rest bits. Such data is not synchronous, since its character rate is random and not externally controlled. Yet, a standard asynchronous data multiplexer cannot process such a 37-bit data character. Such odd data formats can be treated isochronously, however, by multiplexers equipped with an isochronous channel option. A final classification of data which is best treated isochronously is truly synchronous data running at an awkward rate compared to the other modem or trunk rates in the system. For instance, it would be very difficult to find a multiplexer that could multiplex two 1050 bps synchronous terminals on one 2400 bps line. If, however, the data is regarded as isochronous, this combination becomes easier to handle since, as discussed below, the integer fraction relationship no longer governs.

Isochronous Multiplexing Techniques

A descriptive term for an isochronous data multiplexer is a data stuffing multiplexer. Since the incoming data rate is not precisely known, enough trunk capacity is reserved to handle the fastest rate anticipated. If there is not enough data to occupy all of the trunk space reserved (if some box-cars might leave empty), fill bits or characters are inserted as required. The problem in isochronous multiplexing is recognizing this fill data at the receiving end and deleting it from the demultiplexed data stream. There are many techniques available to accomplish this. In some multiplexers a special common channel is used to send error-protected stuffing information for all isochronous channels; or a special bit may be added to each character to signal whether the character is data or fill. In other multiplexers, less trunk capacity than required is assigned to the channel and the excess characters, if any, are sent via another channel of the multiplexer marked with an address. All these techniques call for sophistication in design to prevent error multiplication or severe loss of data due to line noise. Therefore, it is preferable to use isochronous multiplexing only when the more standard synchronous data multiplexing techniques are impossible. Another disadvantage of isochronous multiplexing is that it only rarely can be as efficient as synchronous multiplexing. The fill characters, auxiliary channels, or control bits usually reduce efficiency by 10 to 20%.

Figure 3-10 shows the principal elements of a typical isochronous multiplexer channel. Clock is recovered from the incoming data stream and used to load data into a storage register or memory buffer. Data or fill characters are removed from the memory buffer as required to fill the trunk slots. Upon demultiplexing, the data characters — minus any fill data — are stored in a memory buffer and outputted at a rate deter-

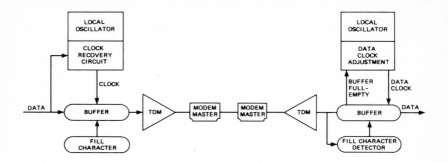

Figure 3-10/Typical Isochronous Data Channel Adaptor for Standard Time Division Multiplexer

mined by the amount of data in storage. If the memory is too sparsely filled, the output clock is automatically slowed. If the memory is overloaded, the output clock speeds up. In this way, the multiplexer can track input data that varies by several per cent from some nominal value. The nominal data rate and the maximum range expected are normally programmable features of these systems.

Wideband Time Division Multiplexers

Wideband line facilities are available from the common carriers to carry data at rates such as 56, 230.4, and 1,544 kbps (T1). Wideband transmission facilities differ from voiceband facilities not only in data rate but also in error rate. The reliability of the wideband services offered by Bell and others is on the average two orders of magnitude better than that found on typical Bell conditioned private-wire lines. This improvement is realized primarily because wideband channels do not require conditioning: They go through fewer PCM and FDM stages during transmission, and are segregated from the crosstalk and impulse noise sources originating from the close proximity of the leased lines to the lines of the dial-up voice network.

46

Wideband multiplexers are ideal vehicles for making efficient use of these reliable transmission facilities. Wideband data usually consists of transmissions between computers or between computers and terminal controllers or remote data concentrators.

The most commonly available wideband multiplexers multiplex synchronous data, either alone or with EIA control signals, and are bit-interleaved. The disadvantages of bit multiplexers discussed earlier in reference to asynchronous data multiplexers (lower efficiency, fewer diagnostics) do not apply in the case of a purely synchronous data multiplexer. Bit-interleaved synchronous data multiplexers are relatively simple and nearly 100% efficient. A bit-interleaved multiplexer is programmed by establishing the number of bits in the frame and then apportioning them among the channels being multiplexed in exact proportion to their speeds. In the true synchronous multiplexer of the type we are describing here, no stuffing bits are used, and an integer fraction relationship exists between the trunk wideband data rate and the multiplexed low-speed channel rates. Also, since there is a practical limit to the number of bits in a frame, the common denominator of all low-speed channel fractions in a system must be less than the largest frame size possible.

Hierarchies of multiplexers may be constructed; an example of such a system is illustrated in Figure 3-11. Incidentally, the cascading of wideband multiplexers, in the same box or in separate cabinets, makes it possible to overcome partially the limitations of frame length, since two TDM's in tandem produce a frame effectively equal to the product of the two frames. In this case, the low-speed rate is equal to the product of two integer fractions. Absolute (i.e., 100%) multiplexing efficiency is not normally possible, since some bits are preempted to establish and monitor channel synchronization. Such diagnostics as local and remote loopback, out-of-sync indicators, test data generator, and error detector and buffer overflow lamps should be provided.

47

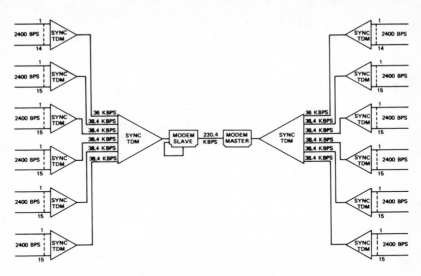

*Figure 3-11/Wideband multiplex hierarchy multiplexes
89 channels of 2400 bps data. Many other combinations,
some using fewer multiplexers, are also possible.*

Wideband TDM's must be provided with a wide variety of
data interfaces. Possible interfaces on the trunk side include
the unipolar coaxial current 303 modem interface used at 50
and 230.4, the DDS balanced bipolar 56 kbps interface, the
CCITT V.35 bipolar interface, and the T1 tri-state interface.
On the low-speed side, EIA and MIL STD interfaces may be
required, in addition to the others mentioned above. Unfortunately, at present there is no standardization on connectors or electrical characteristics, so care must be taken to insure that the interfaces are properly designated at the time
the multiplexer is ordered.

4

Drops and Inserts

MULTIPOINT MULTIPLEXING

Advantages of Multipoint Multiplexing

In the previous chapters we discussed the ways in which point-to-point multiplexing systems can be used to save money and reduce hardware bulk and complexity. Many data communications applications, however, involve a central computer and more than one terminal concentration in remote cities. Figure 4-1 shows how such a system might be configured in the simple point-to-point manner. This system, while better than one not using multiplexers at all, is quite expensive, since it requires one leased line, two modems and two multiplexers for each remote site included in the network. Figure 4-2 shows in idealized form the same network reconfigured for minimum line and hardware costs. The technical advantages and disadvantages to be considered in achieving ideal minimum cost multipoint networks are discussed in this chapter and the next.

Lowest Cost Multipoint System — Round-Robin
Full Duplex from a Simplex Line

The round-robin multipoint system shown in Figure 4-3 is the simplest multipoint system possible. Notice that only one multiplexer and one modem are required at each location and that a 2-wire simplex line is all that is required for complete full-duplex communications. This last statement sounds paradoxical, since a simplex line cannot be expected to support full-duplex communications. However, if we use the freight train analogy again, the principle becomes clear. The train, headed by a sync character engine, leaves city A and heads toward city B. There are enough boxcars in the train to hold all the data waiting on the loading platform at cities B, C, and D. The boxcars are assigned to particular cities and are so labelled. The communication line is a one-way track that the train runs on in a continuous circle. As the train

51

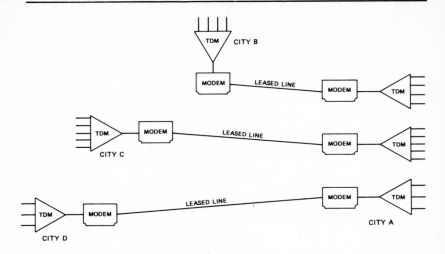

Figure 4-1/Multipoint Network Implemented by Using Point-to-Point Multiplexers. Compare this with the more sophisticated systems of Figures 4-2, 4-3, 4-4, and 4-5.

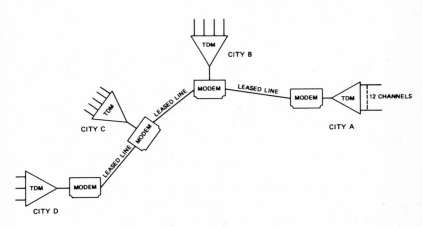

Figure 4-2/Idealized multipoint network saves modems, TDM's, and leased line mileage. Compare with Figure 4-1.

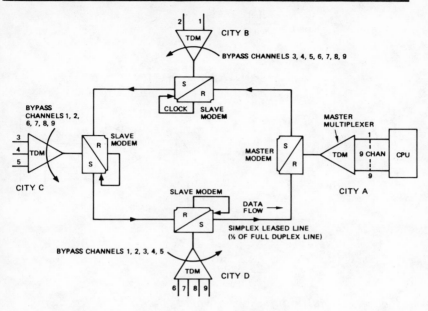

Figure 4-3/Round-Robin Multipoint System — Cities B, C, and D Talking to City A

passes through each city, the boxcars for that city are instantaneously unloaded and loaded so that the train need never stop. The other boxcars pass through undelayed and untouched. At city A all data is unloaded and a new train is formed. Note that if the computer in city A wishes to send data to city D, that data must first pass through cities B and C; if data from city B goes to city A, it must pass through cities C and D. If there is data going between cities D and C, it must be unloaded at city A and put on the next train leaving. In this case, the remote cities are all communicating with the central city (A), but can also talk with each other if a channel card and looping plug, or equivalent, are used at city A, as shown in Figure 4-4.

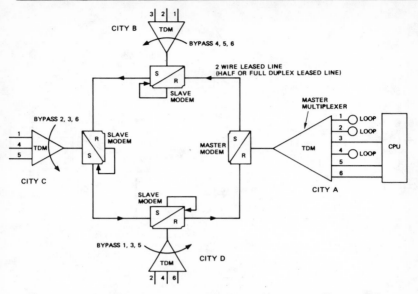

Figure 4-4/Multipoint system where all cities talk to each other.

Normally, only 4-wire full-duplex private lines are furnished by the phone company. The additional two lines can be used for a second, completely different system circulating in the reverse direction, or as a backup loop for the primary system on those occasions (usually rare) when only one pair of the 4-wire line has failed.

Linear Multipoint System

Figure 4-5 shows a 4-wire multipoint configuration, useful where the geographical configuration makes a linear approach more economical in line cost. A send pair of lines and a receive pair must be tied together at each midpoint to complete the loop connection. This connection is best accomplished through a midpoint amplifier, since the loss in a leased line is typically 16 dB; if this is not made up at the midpoint tap,

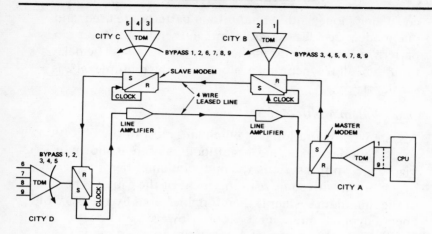

Figure 4-5/Linear Multipoint Multiplexing System Using One Modem per Midpoint Location

the total receive level loss at city A will be 32 dB, resulting in unnecessary data errors. Such amplifiers are available from those TDM manufacturers that offer multipoint systems of this type.

The systems of Figures 4-3 and 4-5 have the advantage of requiring only one modem and one multiplexer at each site; they do not require channel cards or buffers at the remote sites for data which is just passing through, and such passed-through data is not significantly delayed. These advantages have made this, historically, the most popular multipoint TDM system. It does have several disadvantages which have prompted users to modify the basic system in several ways. These disadvantages include the restriction that the modem speed be the same on all links, that remote loopback diagnostics do not function in the normal manner, and the fact that if one section of the line fails, communications between all cities cease. Another disadvantage of the systems using only a single modem at midpoint sites is that, if automatically

equalizing modems that send retrain patterns are used, and
one modem decides to retrain and and sends out its retrain
pattern, all the modems in the loop must retrain. The delay
until they all resynchronize, along with the multiplexers, is
substantial.

Dual Modem Multipoint Systems

A system configuration that eliminates most of the objections
to the round-robin or linear multipoint system is shown in
Figure 4-6. In this system, the midpoint amplifier is replaced
by a modem with some rearrangement of the cables. The cost
of the minimum system is therefore increased by the price of
one modem per midpoint location. However, each section of
the line is used in a normal 4-wire point-to-point mode so
that all modem loopback diagnostics function normally and
each pair of modems can be equalized (or can automatically
equalize) in the normal manner. Another advantage of the
system is that the analog or digital loopback switch on the
midpoint modem can be used as a bypass switch to isolate
city C when a line failure between cities C and B occurs.
Cities A and B can then continue to communicate while the
line between C and B is being repaired. Therefore, many
communications managers feel that the added cost of one
modem is a well-justified expense.

Synchronization of Multipoint Systems

The systems of Figures 4-3, 4-4, 4-5, and 4-6 require that one
modem supply the master clock and that all other modems
be slaved to it. This connection is accomplished at each slave
site by using the modem receive data clock as an external
send clock. (Loop pin 17 to pin 24 and strap the modem for
external clock.) Likewise, each remote site multiplexer must
be strapped to act as a midpoint or slave unit as far as generating its frame is concerned. The necessity for this may be
seen most easily by returning to the train analogy. If, as in
the normal point-to-point system, each multiplexer were free

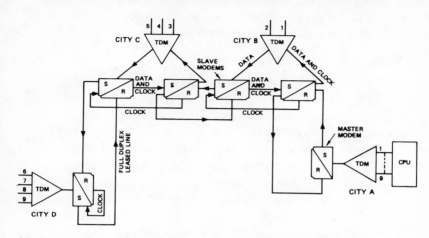

Figure 4-6/Linear multipoint system permits modems to equalize and loopback in pairs.

to generate its own train, it would be necessary to transfer cargo between trains at each stop. This means additional storage and delay since the departure and arrival times of the trains would be random. It is much better if the arriving train and the departing train are the same, or operate in synchronism, so that no appreciable delay occurs and no storage is necessary. This situation is only attainable if the length and velocity of the train is the same on both sides of the midpoint station. Thus the frame lengths and the modem speeds must be identical on both sides of the midpoint remote or endpoint, and the incoming frame sync character must control the generation of the outgoing sync character and frame.

If storage is available, and delay or cost is not a factor, it is always possible to use channel cards or logic at the midpoint locations to provide data buffering and to loop the data at the low-speed connector with a looping plug or strap. Now each link need not be synchronized to the others or even run at the same speed, although in some multiplexers the frame programs must still be the same, since independent receive and send frame patterns are not possible.

Multiplexing Multiplexers

Another solution to the multipoint multiplexing requirement is illustrated in Figure 4-7. In this system, the synchronous aggregate stream is multiplexed by the next multiplexer in the system (equivalent to loading one train onto the flatcars of another, larger train for the remainder of the journey).

The major advantage of this technique is that each leg can run with its own frame programming at the data rate most economical for it. Note, however, that all slower modems must still be synchronized to the master clock of the fastest modem in the system, and that all synchronous data rates must be related by simple integer fractions, such as 1/4, 1/3, 2/3, 1/8, 3/4, etc. Synchronization is required; otherwise, the piggy-back train will not fit exactly on the flatcars reserved for it. Another decided advantage of this system is that a failure of a remote line or modem has no effect on the communications between the higher-level locations. One disadvantage of this system is the requirement for two modems at each midpoint location and two multiplexers per drop point (one at the remote end and one at the central site). Another disadvantage is that the number of times one can remultiplex is limited by the fact that the data rate usually doubles at each remultiplexing. Split-stream modems may be used in these systems without affecting the basic cost or architecture of the system. See Chapter 3 for multipoint systems using split-stream modems.

Multipoint Intercity Contention

To continue the train analogy, let us suppose that a boxcar can be used by any city on a first-come, first-served basis, and that a train of mostly empty cars circulates continuously around the track. As soon as a city has found and loaded

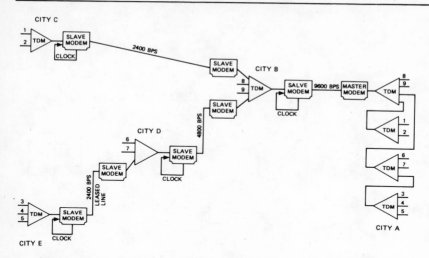

Figure 4-7/The multiplexing of multiplexers permits independent choice of data rates for remote links and prevents general failure due to remote line failure.

an empty boxcar, it marks the outside of it to indicate to the other cities that the boxcar is reserved during this and subsequent trips. When all freight has been transported, an "empty" sign is posted on the boxcar and another shipper is free to put his mark on the boxcar.

Multiplexers with this capability are offered by at least two major TDM manufacturers. The technique is usually referred to as intercity contention and is illustrated in Figure 4-8. If the terminals gain access to the TDM's via the dial network and a phone company rotary, both intercity and intracity contention are possible.

The advantage of this system is that many terminals can share the available multiplexer and computer ports. Also, the contention occurs at the remote location so that the transmission data rate need be no higher than the rate the central computer can handle. RS-232 control signals are used to control the

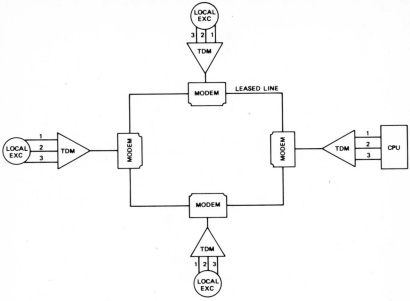

Figure 4-8/Intercity contention option permits several rotary groups to contend for the available computer ports on a first-come first-served basis.

contention process. Thus the raising of "Carrier Detect" or "Data Terminal Ready" signifies a desire to occupy a multiplexer channel. An output such as "Busy-Out" signifies to a would-be user attached to other multiplexers in other cities that the slot is already occupied. (A rotary would move such a caller to the next free channel if one were available.)

Polling Via Multiplexer

In the event that the computer initiates calls to the terminals, its call or poll must be broadcast to all terminals in all cities simultaneously. The terminal recognizing the poll responds by raising a control signal and thereby claims a slot on the multiplexer for its data going back to the computer, as in the multipoint contention system described above. Figure 4-9 shows how several computer polling lines may be multiplexed and distributed to several cities and to several terminal groups within each city. The polling option usually is implemented by straps that signify which channel cards a particular poll is to be broadcast to.

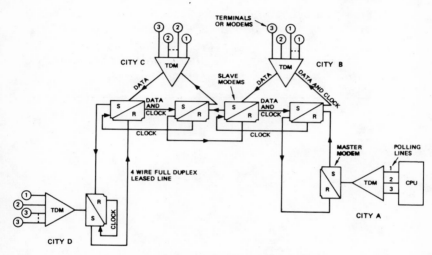

Figure 4-9/Multipoint Polling System. Three computer polling lines are distributed to terminals in three remote cities.

Figure 4-10 shows how two multiplexers, one with a polling feature, can be used to poll co-located terminals when no low-speed modems or phone lines are used. Both TDM's may be reduced to one if a multiple aggregate line unit or other special multiplexer is used. The use of a multiplexer in this application, while unusual, provides the proper connectors, interface isolation, circuit loading, and diagnostic features desirable in such circumstances.

61

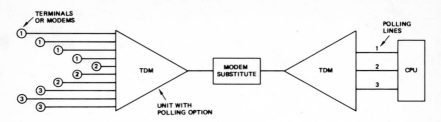

Figure 4-10/Local Polling Signal Distribution and Switching System. Units shown individually may also be obtained in one self-contained package. This system allows computer polling without multidrop telephone lines and modems by simulating such systems for the computer.

5

Multipoint Multiplexing Revisited

Multipoint Multiplexing Revisited

Multitrunk TDM's

In the last chapter we discussed multipoint systems that can be implemented using multiplexers with one aggregate high-speed output line (trunk). In recent years, new TDM's have become available that can process more than one multiplexed data trunk simultaneously. In this chapter, we shall describe the unusual features of such multiplexers and the many systems configurations in which they serve as building blocks.

Multitrunk TDM Features

The true multitrunk time division multiplexer can interface to two or more synchronous high-speed modems, can generate completely independent aggregate frames for each modem, and does not normally require that the modems be clock synchronized to each other. The multitrunk multiplexer can be looked at, functionally, as several independent TDM's sharing the same common logic, buffer memory, power supply, and diagnostics. The sharing of memory is important, since it is the access to a common memory by each trunk line that makes possible the bypassing or feeding through of data from one trunk to another with minimum delay and without the need for channel cards. In the past, some manufacturers have caused confusion by describing as multitrunk TDM's units that simply multiplexed synchronous data. Such units look superficially like multitrunk TDM's because they interface to several synchronous modems, as shown in the last chapter. However, the true test of whether a given multiplexer is a multitrunk unit is not how many synchronous modems are connected, but whether those synchronous channels are trunks or just channels being multiplexed. Questions to ask are — Can multiplexed trunk characters be bypassed easily from one trunk to another? Can one

single trunk multiplexer demultiplex the final aggregate channel at the remote end? (Only one is needed if a true multitrunk TDM is used.)

Drop and Insert Systems

A three-point drop, insert, and bypass system is illustrated in
Figure 5-1. Only one multitrunk TDM is required and it is
used at the midpoint location. In an ideal drop, insert, and
bypass system, each city can communicate with all other
cities; the aggregate bit rates on all trunks are independent
and determined only by the number of channels to be multiplexed on a link; and the failure of one link has no effect on
the others. Channels from city A destined for city C are
passed through city B with a maximum delay of one character time. The delay is necessary if the links are to be truly
independent, since incoming data may arrive just too late to
be loaded in the outgoing frame and must therefore be stored
for one frame before its slot comes around again. If incoming
and outgoing midpoint frames are locked as in the systems of
the previous chapter, it is possible to eliminate the delay; but
then all modems must be locked together and modem or line
failures would bring the whole system down. In the drop and
insert system, only one multiplexer per city is required and
only the midpoint locations require two modems and multitrunk TDM's. There is no serious limitation on the number of
midpoints that may be used in such a system (provided the
accumulated delay is not a problem) since the data is regen-
erated as it is bypassed at each midpoint. In this system, as in
all previous and subsequent ones, when synchronous data
channels are multiplexed, all modems through which the
synchronous data bits pass must be locked together. The
end-point multiplexers need not be special multitrunk units,
but they, of course, must generate a frame and sync pattern
compatible with them.

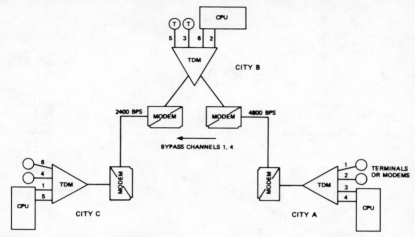

Figure 5-1/Drop and Insert Configuration. Note that lines are independent and that although six pairs of channels are multiplexed no more than four channel cards are required in any multiplexer.

Multitrunk TDM as Terminus

Quite often several remote groups of terminals wish to communicate with a single central computer location. A multi-trunk unit can then serve as several TDM's in one box in a terminus configuration, saving space and hardware cost. Figure 5-2 shows such a system. In principle it is simply three point-to-point networks combined at one end.

The multitrunk TDM may also be used conveniently as the terminal unit in multipoint networks where multiplexers have been multiplexed. In Figure 5-3, the multiplexed data of the low-speed channel from city C is multiplexed again at city B; finally it is demultiplexed twice at city A by feeding the partially demultiplexed aggregate data stream back into a trunk input for demultiplexing the second time. Since this system involves the multiplexing of a synchronous data modem, all but one of the modems must operate in the slave mode.

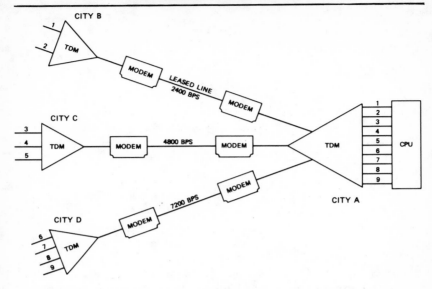

Figure 5-2/Multitrunk Used as Multicity System Terminus. Each line is completely independent of the others.

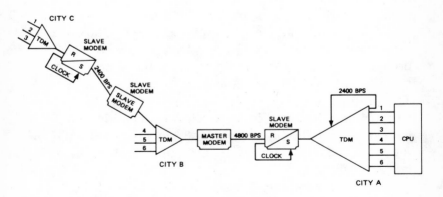

Figure 5-3/Multitrunk Unit Used in Two-Level Multiplexing System. The extra channel cards in the multitrunk unit act as a second multiplexer.

Bypass Capability and the Star Configuration

In the terminus system of Figure 5-2, each aggregate line is demultiplexed at the computer site, and cities B, C, and D cannot talk to each other. If the multitrunk unit could transfer data characters between trunks as well as demultiplex them, a great many multipoint systems would be economically feasible and technically convenient to configure. Furthermore, if several incoming aggregate trunks can be reformatted to form a single outgoing trunk, the multiplexing efficiency of the system may be improved enough to allow a slower-speed modem to be used on that final trunk. For example, three incoming 2400 bps trunks, each 65% utilized, can be reformatted to form one 4800 line, rather than requiring the 7200 that would be necessary if split-stream modems or nested multiplexing were used. Figure 5-4 shows a system illustrating the advantages of the star configuration with reformatting and channel bypass features. Some multiplexers with trunk bypass capability require that the clocks of the trunks bypassed be synchronized. Some multiplexers also have minor restrictions as to the maximum number of channels that can be bypassed and the number of trunks between which they can be switched; sometimes groups of channels being bypassed must have adjacent positions in the frame, or consecutive channel numbers. Bypass programming is usually accomplished on patch pin panels or replaceable ROM's.

Unsynchronized trunk systems are to be preferred, since they may offer a wider choice of trunk data rates and are a little easier to troubleshoot.

In Figure 5-4, even if no terminals are to be multiplexed at city B, a multiplexer can be used as a channel switching device or simply as a convenient diagnostic and control center node from which loopback or fallback procedures can be initiated.

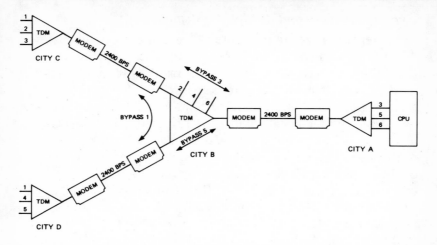

Figure 5-4/Multitrunk Multiplexer at City B with Channel Bypass Capability Permits All Cities to Communicate via Independent Links

Combination Multipoint Network

Figure 5-5 shows a system which combines the multipoint techniques discussed in both this and the previous chapter. This system can be implemented with equipment readily available from today's TDM and modem manufacturers. Multitrunk units are drawn larger, to distinguish them from the simpler point-to-point-type units. The system shown allows terminals in eight cities to communicate over three leased lines (with drops). It is synchronous throughout and could be conveniently implemented via the DDS network when that network extends to all such locations. Depending on the multiplexers used, the modems between city F, city E, and city C may be master modems, particularly if no synchronous data is multiplexed at city F or city E.

70

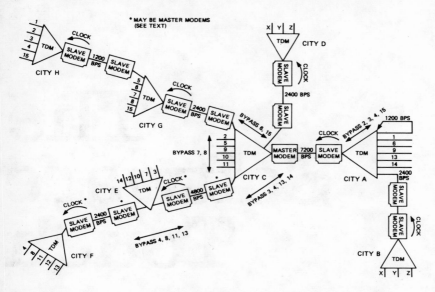

Figure 5-5/This system combines the star, bypass, terminus, drop and insert, and multiplexing multiplexer techniques to provide economical communications between 8 cities.

6

The Software Touch

SOFTWARE MULTIPLEXING AND TDM'S AS INEXPENSIVE COMPUTER FRONT ENDS

Advantages of Multiplexing in Software

In the systems discussed previously it has always been assumed that the multiplexed channels would be demultiplexed by a matching multiplexer before going into the ports of the front end of a computer. But front ends are, in some ways, another form of multiplexer — one that converts serial start-stop or synchronous data from many ports to a multiplexed format suitable for transfer to the mainframe. So why demultiplex just in order to remultiplex in a front end? Why not input the aggregate character-interleaved stream through a single front-end serial data interface adapter and let the computer sort out the received data and format the send data?

Actually, this idea is almost as old as time division multiplexing itself and is one of the early reasons why character-interleaved multiplexers were favored over bit-interleaved units. In deciding whether software multiplexing is appropriate in a given system, several items should be considered. First, it must be determined if the cost per port of the computer front end is less than that of the TDM which is replacing it. And secondly, if a TDM is used, can it be remotely located and serve as an inexpensive remote concentrator? In the system of Figure 6-1, the multiplexer is used as a substitute for some of the front-end hardware and no aggregate long-distance transmission line is involved. To the extent that TDM hardware is less expensive than CPU front-end ports, a significant saving can often be realized. In the case of some mini- or micro-computers there may be no choice since an adequate front end may not be available. The cost of writing the program to multiplex and demultiplex (usually a one man-month effort) must be assessed, as must the amount of computer

73

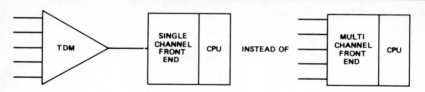

Figure 6-1/Often, a character-interleaved time division multiplexer is more economical than a multiport computer front end.

capacity in memory and processing time the software multiplexing may require, compared to the processing time required to control a standard multiported front end.

In Figure 6-2 the multiplexer serves as a remote concentrator; the saving in hardware by software multiplexing is greater because no multiplexer is required at the computer end. Split-stream modems rather than multiplexers may also be used in this application although, since the split-stream modems are bit-interleaved, the software is more complex and the computer time required is usually greater. Also, since split-stream modems do not normally use frame sync bits, channel identification must be determined by the CPU after examination of the demultiplexed data streams, and character formation must be performed in the CPU rather than in the front end.

Some modems and at least one multiplexer have been equipped with IBM-compatible parallel bus interfaces and so could interface directly to host processors, entirely eliminating the need for 270X- or 370X-type front ends. In this case, the TDM is indistinguishable from a standard CPU front end for many applications, but is available at a significantly lower price.

Figure 6-2/A Character-Interleaved Time Division Multiplexer Used as a Remote Concentrator

Asynchronous Software Multiplexing

There are basically two types of computer front end communications interfaces — asynchronous and synchronous. Asynchronous ports (teletype adapters) are usually the least expensive and simplest with which to work. They require start-stop characters; therefore, if a TDM is to gain access to a computer via an asynchronous front-end port it must look asynchronous and put a start bit and a rest bit on each aggregate trunk character. In asynchronous software demultiplexing, the front end strips the start and stop bits and transfers eight-bit characters to the central processor. In asynchronous software demultiplexing, the CPU software must find the frame synchronization character as well as sort out the multiplexed data, though the bits of each character are preassembled by the front end.

One of the disadvantages of asynchronous software demultiplexing is the difficulty of clocking the system when only standard equipment is available. If much data is to be multiplexed, a fairly high trunk data rate is necessary; but async computer ports rarely operate at speeds higher than 9600 bps, so a special speed option may be required. Even if a higher-speed option is obtainable from the computer manufacturer, the port must be clockable externally or output its clock to drive the multiplexer. The reason for this restriction is that almost all multiplexers are synchronous, externally clocked devices and cannot recover clock from an input aggregate data stream, even if such a stream has start and stop bits. Thus, in the absence of a pair of modems between the TDM and the computer, either the computer must lend its clock to the multiplexer or an external auxiliary oscillator must be used to drive both multiplexer and computer (Figure 6-3). When synchronous modems are interposed (Figure 6-4), the computer must be modified so that it can either use the modem transmit clock to output data, or clock the modem from its own internal oscillator. If asynchronous modems (202's) are used between the multiplexer and the computer (Figure 6-5), then a clock oscillator and recovery circuit must be provided at the TDM end to generate receive and send clocks to operate the multiplexer. The result expected of these options is that the data appear synchronous to the multiplexer and asynchronous to the computer. In addition to requiring start and stop bits on each character, both the computer and the TDM must output their characters continuously head to tail.

Synchronous Software Multiplexing

The use of a synchronous computer port connected to a remote TDM via a synchronous modem and line is quite common. Synchronous ports usually cost considerably more than asynchronous ports but the clocking problem is simplified, since both the computer and the TDM are operating as they usually do in that regard. Most hardware front ends search for the sync character in the data stream and require both a particular sync character and at least two sync characters in a row. Therefore a multiplexer used with such a computer should have the option of providing double sync characters and varying the character used. In some front ends the sync characters are deleted before data is transferred to the main frame memory. In such a case it is essential that an additional and different frame sync or other character be put in each frame so that the main frame software is able to identify the

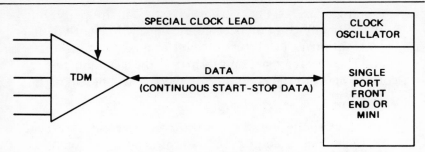

Figure 6-3/Asynchronous Data Software Multiplexing Without a Modem Using a Standard Synchronous Trunk TDM

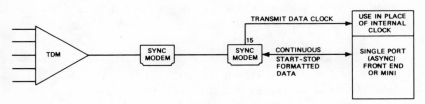

Figure 6-4/Asynchronous Software Multiplexing via Synchronous Modems Using an Asynchronous Front-End Port

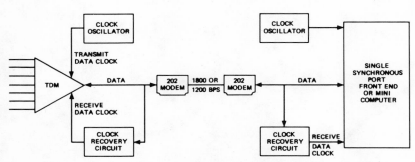

Figure 6-5/Synchronous Software Multiplexing via 202 Modems Using a Synchronous Front-End Port

beginning of each frame and sort out the data properly. In addition, many computers can only work with eight-bit characters, but many TDM's use nine-bit or mixed byte size formats. The character size and format of the TDM must be compatible with the computer to which it will be talking.

Programming for Software Multiplexing

While it is beyond the scope of this book to go into the specific algorithms or coding used in typical systems, some general principles can be suggested. It is the responsibility of the program to insure that the character rate in a particular channel is not exceeded even on a short-term basis. Thus, characters for a particular slot must be interspersed periodically with idle or control characters. For example, if a particular frame contains twenty slots per second for a given fifteen character-per-second terminal, one out of every four characters should be idle, rather than sending fifteen consecutive data characters followed by five consecutive idle characters. Sub-routines that can be employed to keep track of when idle characters are due for insertion and the use of slot maps and tables in memory have proven to be effective program approaches.

7

Multiplexers with Minds of Their Own

Multiplexers with Minds of Their Own

The recent introduction of low-cost mini-computers, micro-computers, and micro-processors has encouraged the multi-plexer industry to develop highly sophisticated and versatile time-division multiplexers. These new muxes not only have enough intelligence and memory to operate effectively in the most complex time-sharing or common-carrier environ-ments, but, for the smaller user, the "smart" multiplexers mean greater efficiency, more flexibility in system configu-ration, easier installation, simplified or automatic configura-tion control, remote trouble diagnosis, and error and traffic monitoring reports. Several different types of intelligent multiplexers have reached the market and more are on the way. In this chapter we indicate the capabilities they (will) have.

The intelligent multiplexer with either a special-purpose processor or a standard minicomputer uses stored program software techniques rather than the hard-wired logic of the older generation of TDM's. The use of the software approach means that functions requiring adaptation or flexibility can be more easily implemented, and that special-purpose TDM's can be created faster and at lower cost, than by the logic de-sign method, which requires many board layouts and long cycles of prototyping. It also means that a really flexible basic unit, which consists of a computer, its memory, and its channel interface cards, can look like a time division mul-tiplexer, a concentrator, or an inverse multiplexer, depend-ing on the software installed.

Improved Framing Techniques

One of the major inconveniences of the typical hardware multiplexer is the difficulty of both calculating an efficient frame and then programming the multiplexer for it. Frequent or daily changing of the frame is impractical in most hard-wired TDM's because it must be done manually with special plugs or straps. Therefore one of the earliest uses of read-only memories and simple processors in multiplexers was to store several alternate frame programs and permit them to be switched in and out electronically, either locally or from a central control point. This facility made it possible to lower the aggregate rate when line quality dropped or to alter the mix of channel speeds and codes when processing applications changed during the business day. The ability to shift gears in this way allowed the available aggregate bandwidth to be used more efficiently more of the time. However, where the mix of channels changed every few minutes, as in timesharing applications, the techniques was ineffective. New frames could be loaded into the multiplexers by a computer, a substantial software effort on the part of the CPU owner and a non-volatile read-write frame memory (lest a power glitch erase the stored frame information) would be required.

Two basic techniques — described below—can be used to construct multiplexers that are more efficient than the standard TDM's so far described in this book, and which do not rely on the host computer for dynamic framing decisons. These two techniques are called "statistical framing" and "adaptive framing."

Statistical Techniques in Multiplexer Framing

The most sophisticated statistical framing method avoids the frame concept entirely and sends data in blocks or packets. This method, usually referred to as "statistical multiplexing," should be called "probability multiplexing," since it gambles on the fact that in most systems, many terminals and computers will be idle enough of the time to make room for additional channels. In a straightforward statistical multiplexer for asynchronous data, the characters to be multiplexed are first buffered and then sent, using a synchronous block format similar to SDLC or BISYNC, with header characters indicating which characters belong to which channels. The length of these blocks need not be fixed but are usually long enough to completely empty the channel buffers of any characters stored since the last block was sent. Each block must have some means of error control, particularly for that part of the format which tells to which channels the characters in this block belong. Obviously, a header error could cause garbling of an entire block in a statistical multiplexer; therefore, error control is essential in statistical multiplexers. The usual error-control technique is ARQ (Automatic Request for Retransmission) of a block found to be in error.

While somewhat more expensive to implement than fixed-frame TDM's, statistical multiplexers can double or even triple line usage. There are drawbacks to the technique, however; as channels become more active, the multiplexing delay increases. The delay also increases if a noisy aggregate line requires frequent block retransmissions. Since the amount of channel character buffering is limited, actual buffer overflow and loss of data may occur if channel activity and the error rate combine adversely. Quite large amounts of buffer memory may be required to avoid overflow, particularly at the computer end multiplexer, where several computer ports may become active at once and send pages of data without pause. Thus the decision to use a statistical multiplexer of this type must be made both by comparing the cost of the feature with the value of the increased trunk capacity obtained and by carefully evaluating the probabilities of data activity and the effects of increased multiplexing delay. Note that because of header and error control overhead, it is possible for a statistical multiplexer to be less efficient than a fixed-frame unit if the channels being multiplexed are unusually active or full duplex.

Another problem for statistical multiplexers is the handling of synchronous data. Since blocks are sent irregularly, vary in size, and may be interrupted by retransmissions, it is virtually impossible to maintain true synchronous data transmission through the multiplexer. If the synchronous channel data is not encrypted and uses a standard block transmission protocol such as Bisync, it is possible to take each Bisync block as it comes, buffer it, and then reblock the data as required. Because Bisync and similar protocols are half duplex, a considerable amount of aggregate bandwidth may be made available.

However, remember that the bandwidth conserved may be available in only one direction, particularly in batch systems. Because the statistical multiplexing of synchronous data is protocol sensitive, and the logic and memory required is difficult to get on standard size channel cards, some statistical units split the aggregate bandwidth between the synchronous and statistical sections of the multiplexer and essentially revert to the fixed-frame mode for synchronous data.

Data Compression Techniques

Efficiency in intelligent multiplexers may also be improved by code translation techniques. For example, if an ASCII-coded terminal sends only numeric characters, only four of the normal eight data bits need by multiplexed for that channel. If necessary, escape codes can be used to shift between alpha-numeric data multiplexing and the foreshortened mode. Other opportunities for data compression exist where only upper-case letters are used. For instance, conversion from ASCII to Baudot code before multiplexing can save two bits per character and therefore increase channel capacity by about 25%. Incidentally, several such converters are available for less than the cost of a basic TDM channel card. It is also possible to convert the full ASCII code set to a new format where the number of bits assigned to each character depends on the frequency with which the character is used. Character lengths of three to as many as fourteen bits are used. The numbers and frequently-used control characters or letters such as E and the other vowels are assigned the shorter lengths of 3, 4, or 5 bits. The letters Z or Q may be relegated to the 14-bit level. When strings of such variable-length characters are assembled in a frame, it is not easy to tell where one character ends and the next begins. Start and stop bits are of no use here and would impact efficiency adversely. It turns out, however, that if certain rules are used to assign the bit patterns to the ASCII characters, the translated characters become self-delineating. The basic principle here is that many bit patterns are declared illegal. Thus, if the letter E is 001,

84

then 0011 is defined as E followed by the first bit of the next character, but 0010 is recognized as the first four bits of some other character.

Such code translation techniques can double multiplexing efficiency, but also are difficult and expensive to implement. For one thing, if the multiplexer handles a mixture of Baudot-, IBM- and ASCII- coded channels, multiple code translation ROM's are required; they must be assigned to the proper channels, either manually by straps, or dynamically, as channels sign on and indicate what code they are using. It is also clear that even a single bit error in transmission will cause a loss of character synchronization and a multiplication of errors. Therefore, error control is absolutely essential in a data compression system. Error control implies a block transmission format, so data compression technique is pretty much limited to intelligent multiplexers. When both the data compression technique and the statistical framing systems are combined, some startling improvements in efficiency are possible, particularly in manual teletype message-switching systems.

The data compression technique may be used efficiently in a fixed-frame mode as well. For instance, an empty channel slot can be represented by a two-bit character. Thus, empty frame slots are made as small as possible to keep efficiency high, but each frame has the same number of characters and each frame slot belongs to a particular channel. Such a multiplexer must of course be programmed by hand with slots assigned in proportion to channel speed, but this method eliminates the need to put a long header on each frame to indicate which channel gets which characters. As with purely statistical multiplexers, problems arise when synchronous data is multiplexed in such a variable length frame unit. As before, synchronous data is handled by recognition of the protocol characters and re-blocking of the data.

Adaptive Framing

A most effective technique to improve efficiency in dynamic situations without incurring the risks of statistical multiplexing or the costs of data compression is to use a multiplexer that periodically adjusts its frame based on the channels connected to it. Such an adaptive framing multiplexer is a fixed-frame multiplexer that can modify its frame as necessary whenever a channel signs on and indicates its desire to transmit by raising a control signal or sending a character. Installation of such a multiplexer requires little more than connecting channel cables and turning on the power, particularly if the multiplexer also has an adaptive speed capability (see below). The adaptively framing TDM allots the available frame characters to the low-speed channels as they sign on in proportion to their speed until all aggregate slots are used up. Late callers get busy signals or busy messages. As users hang up, their frame slots are automatically re-allocated to new callers. Channels in such a TDM may be framed or dropped, depending on the states of such EIA control signals as Data Terminal Ready, Carrier Detect, or Request to Send. Remote and central TDM's adapt themselves regardless of the location at which an incoming channel first makes an appearance. It is never necessary to go off-line or to intervene manually to change the frame of any multiplexer in a system.

The advantages of an adaptively framing multiplexer are that large data buffers are not required, buffer overflow is not possible, the units are code transparent and can handle synchronous data or encrypted data, and the multiplexing delay is stable and comparable to that of fixed-frame multiplexers. The adaptive multiplexer can offer, but does not inherently need, error control since it is sensitive to errors only on those relatively rare occasions when the TDM's are shifting to a new frame.

The adaptive framing technique is extremely efficient in dial-up systems or where Request to Send or Data Terminal Ready is lowered for a substantial period of time. In the case where a terminal is used only an hour a day, it is clear that the

86

many hours of empty slots saved can be improved upon only slightly by saving the occasional empty slots during the active hour.

The automatically framing multiplexer can also adapt to changes in the aggregate data rate, further relieving the operator of programming chores. Both statistical and dynamic framing multiplexers generate network statistics to indicate what percentage of the trunk is being used or to report when the system blocks. At least one intelligent TDM allows the user to partition each aggregate line so that channels may be multiplexed statistically, adaptively, or with a fixed frame all at the same time.

Speed/Code Detection

A major advantage of software multiplexing is the ability to examine the data stream in detail, and respond to what is observed. Speed/code detection is the most difficult data-based decision that an automated TDM must make. In the simple approaches, special preordained characters must be sent, in order for a proper decision to be made. A better approach, which requires no special system tailoring, is to make the decision based on any first character that is received. The decision is made by analysis of transmission times, rest bit appearance, type of parity, and start bit width. This first character is stored and multiplexed after analysis so that the sign-on procedure need be no different for a terminal directly connected to a computer than for one going through a multiplexer. Other reasons for examining the data stream, such as routing, are discussed in the chapter on concentrators.

The Intelligent TDM in Multipoint Systems

In multipoint systems, such as stars and hubs, the new generation of computer-controlled TDM's can automatically format data for several trunk lines at the same time and — without channel cards, patch panels, or straps — bypass data between aggregate lines with minimum delay. Configuration or reconfiguration of multipoint systems requires only the insertion of channel cards at the drop locations and connection of the modems or terminals to them. This alteration is accomplished by search procedures under software control that find equivalent channel addresses. When a data source that has no mate in the network signs on, an alarm goes on.

Automatic Fallback and Enhanced Diagnostics

The adaptive framing TDM calculates its frame and knows its channel capacity by recognizing the aggregate data rate. Should the modem speed be altered so that not all the low-speed channels can be accommodated, the TDM automatically reframes, dropping those channels that have a low priority.

Since software design makes it relatively easy to generate and receive diagnostic status characters, the new multiplexers are able to furnish a central site operator with complete reports of alarms from all remote units, and can facilitate the transmission or receipt of loopback requests, fallback commands, and error-test data to and from all units and channels in the system. TDM processors can likewise use their spare time to run diagnostic routines on their own logic, memory, and peripherals. Thus the new breed of TDM can diagnose their own problems with far greater ease and less cost than can the more traditional multiplexers. Automatic switchover to standby central processors and/or memories is also more effective because of this self-diagnostic capability.

Other Possible Options and Error Control

The flexibility of the software approach makes it possible to conceive of many useful options which could be made available once the intelligent mux becomes commonplace. The formatting of aggregate data according to the bi-sync, DDCMP, or SDLC line protocols makes software demultiplexing a more attractive technique. Automatic dial network fallback and al-

ternate line or modem selection are also system features closely related to an error detection capability. Telex data multiplexing units are also possible.

Those with a large inventory of hardware multiplexers can,
in some cases, use them in concert with the new TDM's, although some efficiency and adaptability is lost. Add-on forward
acting error detection and correction boxes are available for
use with any type of multiplexer and go between the multiplexer and the modem. (See *Basic Techniques in Data Communications*). Whether internal or external to a TDM, the
error control bits take about one-sixth of the aggregate
bandwidth.

By varying the error correcting code used and the block size,
both the transmission delay and the fraction of the aggregate
bandwidth required can be optimized for a particular application. Newer units combine forward error-correction techniques with block retransmission methods and thereby reduce the average transmission delay in this type of error control system.

8
The
Power of
Concentration

There is probably more confusion about the distinction between multiplexing and concentration than there is about almost any other topic in data communications. The word "concentrator" is often loosely applied to time division multiplexers, but in this book the term "concentrator" is reserved for devices which feature contention and/or process or modify data in some fashion. A concentrator with contention is, in its simplest form, a switch with enough skill to connect on demand any of M inputs to a lesser number of N outputs (M-to-N concentrator). Therefore, a system with six CRT's and only four computer ports will need a concentrator where $M = 6$ and $N = 4$. Figure 8-1 illustrates such a basic concentrator. In this system, each CRT contends with the others for the available computer ports on a first-come, first-served basis. By contrast, a pair of time division multiplexers connects all input terminals to the computer all the time.

The Port-Sharing Concentrator

In the simplest type of concentrator, several inputs contend for only one output ($N = 1$). The most common application for such a device is in port- or modem-sharing usage. In Figure 8-2(a), the remote terminals communicate with the computer via modems and a concentrator. The presence of "Modem Carrier" indicates to the concentrator which terminal has initiated a call and is to be through-connected. Alternatively, the computer can initiate the connection by polling the remote terminals, and when one responds by telling its modem to send "Carrier", the concentrator knows which line has responded and can connect it to the computer port. Note that port- or modem-sharing concentrators usually have a broadcast feature which permits a computer polling signal to be sent out on all lines simultaneously. Figure 8-2(b) shows the same concentrator used to permit several terminals to access the same modem. In this case, modems and transmission lines are saved, as well as computer ports. Combinations of local and remote terminals may also share a computer port, as illustrated in Figure 8-2(c). In two of these systems, particular

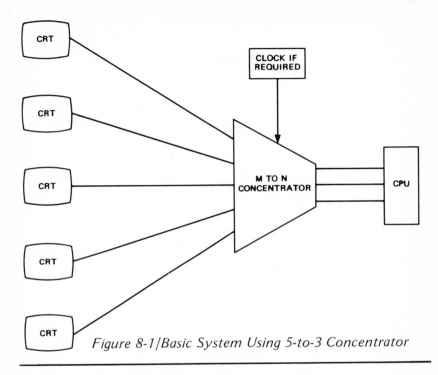

Figure 8-1/Basic System Using 5-to-3 Concentrator

attention must be paid to the clocking if synchronous modems and terminals are involved, and if the broadcast mode is needed. In the case where a local terminal is connected directly to the computer via the concentrator, provision must be made to clock the terminal and computer, as illustrated. These applications usually require special cable adapters or straps in the concentrator to implement, and may also require clock drivers if the modem is unable to support all the clock loads directly.

Simple port-sharing devices usually do not use memory and therefore do not delay or store data. Essentially, transfer connections are made instantaneously and such concentrators are speed-transparent and therefore need no speed or code programming.

Figure 8-2

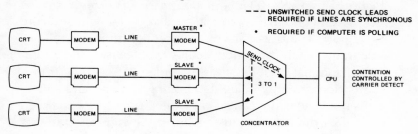

(a)/Port-Sharing Concentrator

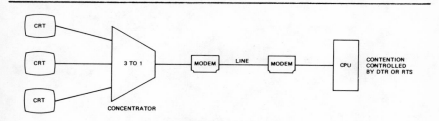

(b)/Modem-Sharing Concentrator

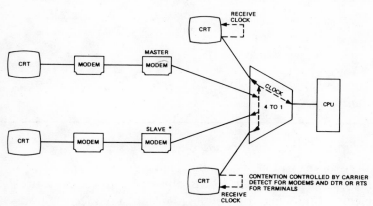

(c)/Hybrid-Sharing Concentrator

Analog Contention

Figure 8-3 shows a telephone-line sharing device. In this device, several phone lines can share a single modem and computer port. The advantage of doing contention on the line side, rather than the digital side, is that fewer modems are required and dial back-up is easily implemented. This form of contention can only be used in polling systems, and all modems must be of the carrier-controlled type, since the presence of carrier is what causes a line to be connected to the modem. In the send direction, all the lines broadcast the same signal.

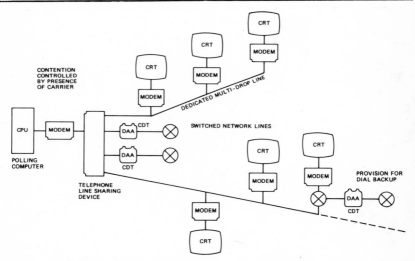

Figure 8-3/Analog Contention Unit Saves Modems in Polling Systems

Combining Concentrators and Multiplexers

Concentrators can be placed between a multiplexer and a computer front end, but it is usually better to concentrate before multiplexing, if possible, in order to reduce the transmission bandwidth and save as many TDM channel cards as possible. Figure 8-4 shows an interesting application using

The Power of Concentration

dial network rotaries, multiplexers, and several simple 4-to-1 concentrators. The system illustrated permits any terminal in any city to dial a local call and be connected to the computer if a port is free. Once all the ports are occupied, the caller receives a busy signal. The intercity contention is performed by the concentrators at the computer. The intra-city contention is handled by phone company free-line-hunting equipment. Note that the modems used at the remote sites must have the capability of looking busy to the central office in response to an EIA level control signal (out-of-service pin 25) from the multiplexer. This signal is generated by the concentrators and applied to the unselected inputs.

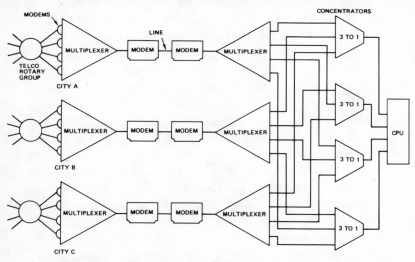

Figure 8-4/A combination of multiplexers and concentrators provides economical interstate and intra-city contention.

Large-Scale M-to-N Concentrators

So far we have discussed concentrators with only a single port (N = 1). Such concentrators have little common logic and cost much less than most modems. Where N is greater than 1, a more substantial device is required.

95

Let us consider the steps required to service a request for a connection in a typical concentrator. The line requesting service first raises a control signal, such as "Ring Indicator" or "Carrier", if a modem, or "Data Terminal Ready" or "Request to Send", if a terminal. The M-to-N concentrator is continually scanning its input lines, looking for an appearance of these signals. When such a request is found, the address of the channel is noted in a memory. A search is now made for a free computer port by scanning a memory containing the present status of the ports. When a free port is found, its address is matched with the address of the input line and stored in memory. Now each time an active input line is scanned, data and control signals can be transferred. Most M-to-N concentrators use circulating shift registers as memory elements, and the number of transfers of data per second are limited by the speed at which the memory can be scanned and the number of lines in the system. Sampling times between five and seventy microseconds are typical; the faster units can operate well at data rates of up to 9600 bps. The sampling technique eliminates the need for speed/code programming in concentrators and permits either synchronous or asynchronous data to be switched.

Almost all M-to-N concentrators also have provision for forming several subcontention groups. This facility permits lines or ports to be grouped by speed or code. Where synchronous data modems are concentrated, provision must be made to transfer clocks as well as data and control signals. If synchronous data terminals are concentrated, a means of clocking the terminals and computer ports must be provided. This is most conveniently done if the concentrator has an oscillator and a clock buss system built in.

Current loop lines may also be concentrated if the concentrator can recognize an idle to active line data transition. The problem here is to determine when disconnect is desired. This problem can be solved, in some cases, by using an EIA interface on the computer side so that the computer can initiate a disconnect by lowering "Data Terminal Ready." Such a concentrator may also be used as an interface converter by setting M equal to N.

Large M-to-N concentrators usually contain displays that make it possible to see which channels are connected to which ports. Switches are also provided to take input lines or output ports temporarily out of service.

More Sophisticated Concentrators

While simple contention-type M-to-N concentrators that respond to control signals have many applications, they are naturally limited to concentration functions that can be performed without examining or reading the data stream or generating characters to be outputted. Some useful functions that one might like a data-inspecting concentrator to perform include port partitioning based on speed or code, and port or computer selection based on application. The ability of a concentrator to generate data characters permits "Busy" messages to be sent to locked-out terminals. Both hardware- and software-based concentrators provide all or some of these data-stream dependent features. Elaborate software concentrators go so far in this direction that they become circuit switches or terminal controllers and perform such functions as polling, data compression, backward or forward error correction, and code conversion. Discussion of such devices, which are loosely called remote concentrators, is beyond the scope of this book.

To perform the data-derived functions enumerated above, the sophisticated concentrator must determine or be told the speed and code of the lines contending. As in adaptive multiplexers, a special first character, usually carriage return or circle D, must be sent by the terminal. The multiplexer or concentrator samples the character, using a convenient clock such as 300 BPS or 600 BPS, and decodes the result — which will be distorted in a predictable fashion if the data is actually, for example, 300, 150, 134.5 or 110. Once the speed is known, the code can be inferred. Additional characters then can be used to indicate alternate codes or to select a particular computer port group. Of course, once the speed and code of a terminal are known, it is possible to send the terminal a "Busy" message. Software-based concentrators are much more flexible in this regard and can send "Busy" messages that include a number representing a terminal's position in a queue. Priority schemes of various types are also available so that special channels can be put at the head of the queue or even interrupt a connection already established. Channel usage reports can also be generated.

The ultimate in data-controlled software concentrators, as in multiplexers, is the concentrator that can adapt automatically without requiring special characters. Such units have almost no limitations on the speeds and codes which can be adaptively concentrated or routed, and do not require terminal operators to use complex sign-on procedures.

By combining concentration with multiplexing, remote concentration operating over a single communications line becomes possible. Such combinations are less expensive and more flexible if done using software techniques, and the distinction between concentrators, multiplexers and remote terminal controllers becomes blurred.

Contention Control and Interfacing

An M-to-N concentrator, like a multiplexer, must appear to be either a modem or a terminal, depending on the device it is attached to. On the output port side, its connectors are usually configured to look like a modem, so that the computer cables may be directly attached. On the line side, the unit looks like a terminal so that modems may be directly attached. Unfortunately, the application of these units varies a great deal, and quite often local terminals contend directly with remote terminals on dial-up or leased lines. In the modem-sharing application, as shown in Figure 8-2(b), terminals seek a single modem and so the concentrator must look like a modem to the terminals and a terminal to the modem.

The Power of Concentration

In most concentrators, the same twisted cable adapters are often required, as illustrated in the following chapter on interfacing to multiplexers. However, the problem in concentrators is compounded by the fact that a control signal is required to make and break the connections. If a modem on a dial-up line is requesting service, it will raise "Ring Indicator." If the modem is on a dedicated line, it will raise "Carrier Detect" to initiate a connection. If a terminal requests service, it will raise "Data Terminal Ready," or if DTR is on all the time, a switchable "Request to Send" may have to be used. To drop a connection, the computer port may lower "Data Terminal Ready," or the connection may have to be disconnected on the line side by a modem lowering "Carrier Detect," or, if half duplex, "Data Set Ready." A terminal may disconnect by lowering DTR or RTS. If data sources are mixed, it may be necessary to use a combination of these methods to operate. Most concentrators rarely make adequate provision to accommodate all these variations, and special cabling or strapping is often required. Some full-duplex terminals in non-polled systems that have no variable control signals can only be concentrated by turning off power to them or their associated modems, or by using a software concentrator.

9

To Each
Its Own

FREQUENCY DIVISION MULTIPLEXING

If time division multiplexing can be thought of as serial multiplexing, then frequency division multiplexing (FDM) is parallel multiplexing. The train analogy that we have been using in the other chapters is strained a great deal here, but still applies if it can be imagined that every freight shipper has his own private track and train and that the freight is shipped as quickly as it is received. FDM was the first widely used multiplexing technology; although it is losing ground to the newer digital techniques, it still probably will be employed extensively as long as analog channels continue to be used to transmit voice traffic.

FDM Basics

The bandwidth of a typical leased line in the United States is about 3 kHz, or from 350 to 3350 Hz; it may be divided into subchannels of smaller bandwidth. Then each subchannel may be used independently of the others in any way desired. The bandwidth needed for a subchannel is a function of the amount of information to be put through it. Speech signals usually require the whole 3000 Hz for intelligibility, but a 50 baud teletype signal may be sent quite comfortably within a 78 Hz voice channel. A lot of 78 Hz channels fit within a 3000 Hz voice channel. Of course, the faster the data rate, the wider the needed channel. Thus a 300 baud channel needs about 420 Hz.

The function of a frequency division multiplexer is to translate the digital data it receives from the data sources being multiplexed into analog signals or tones that fit into the channel bandwidths assigned to them, and to combine them into an aggregate line signal. There are many ways to accomplish this end. For instance, a carrier centered in each channel could be amplitude-modulated by the data or keyed on and off; but analysis has shown that such techniques waste bandwidth and are susceptible to line noise. A method known

as frequency shift keying (FSK) has long been the mainstay
of FDM; there is virtually universal agreement that this form
of frequency modulation yields the optimum combination
of noise immunity, narrow and well-defined bandwidth, and
ease of implementation. In FSK, one frequency represents a
data space, another represents a mark. Each FSK channel
does have a nominal center frequency which can be called
the channel carrier frequency, but since the data is always at
either mark or space, the carrier is almost never observable
at its nominal center frequency.

FDM Families

The ability of an FDM demodulator to separate channel carriers once they have been combined into an aggregate signal
is dependent on the quality of the filters and frequency dis-
criminators used. In earlier years, when filter design was not
as advanced, and modern, stable, solid-state components were
not available, carriers could not be placed as close together as
they now can be. Thus, as the technology developed over the
years, several standard families of channel parameters were
promulgated by various organizations and manufacturers. For
easy reference, four of the most important are shown in
Tables 9-1 through 9-4. Each family defines a channel number, a center frequency, a data rate, and the frequency shift
between mark and space. Equipment from different manufacturers is compatible if it adheres to one of the standard
channel families.

The choice of a family for a particular application often depends on the configuration of the system. In a perfect FDM
system, the amplitude of each channel is the same, and, in
point-to-point systems, this situation is easy to maintain.
Therefore a narrower channel with a broader, less expensive
filter is adequate. In a multi-drop system where signals at remote locations are bridged across a common line, or in dial-
up instances, the amplitudes of the carriers within the composite

Channel Number	75 baud Chan. Spacing 120 Hz FSK ± 30 Hz	150 baud Chan. Spacing 240 Hz FSK ± 60 Hz	600 baud Chan. Spacing 1440 Hz FSK ± 240 Hz
1	420	480	1080
2	540	720	2520
3	660	960	
4	780	1200	
5	900	1440	
6	1020	1680	
7	1140	1920	
8	1260	2160	
9	1380	2400	
10	1500	2640	
11	1620	2880	
12	1740	3120	
13	1860		
14	1980		
15	2100		
16	2220		
17	2340		
18	2460		
19	2580		
20	2700		
21	2820		
22	2940		
23	3060		
24	3180		
25	5300		

Table 9-1/CCITT Operating Frequencies

Channel Number	50/56 baud Chan. Spacing 78 Hz FSK ± 23 Hz	75 baud Chan. Spacing 100 Hz FSK ± 30 Hz	110 baud Chan. Spacing 150 Hz FSK ± 45 Hz
1	397	410	415
2	475	510	565
3	553	610	715
4	631	710	865
5	709	810	1015
6	787	910	1165
7	865	1010	1315
8	943	1110	1465
9	1021	1210	1615
10	1099	1310	1765
11	1177	1410	1915
12	1255	1510	2065
13	1333	1610	2215
14	1411	1710	2365
15	1489	1810	2515
16	1567	1910	2665
17	1645	2010	2815
18	1723	2110	2965
19	1801	2210	3115
20	1879	2310	3265
21	1957	2410	
22	2035	2510	
23	2113	2610	
24	2191	2710	
25	2269	2810	
26	2347	2910	
27	2425	3010	
28	2503	3110	
29	2581	3210	
30	2659	3310	
31	2737		
32	2815		
33	2893		
34	2971		
35	3049		
36	2127		
37	3205		
38	3283		

134.5 baud Chan. Spacing 187 Hz FSK ± 55 Hz	150 baud Chan. Spacing 200 Hz FSK ± 60 Hz	300 baud Chan. Spacing 420 Hz FSK ± 120 Hz	Channel Number
439	410	600	1
626	610	1080	2
813	810	1560	3
1000	1010	2040	4
1187	1210	2520	5
1374	1410	3000	6
1561	1610		7
1748	1810		8
1935	2010		9
2122	2210		10
2309	2410		11
2496	2610		12
2683	2810		13
2870	3010		14
3057	3210		15
3244			16

Table 9-2/Narrowband Operating Frequencies

Channel Number	75 baud Chan. Spacing 170 Hz FSK ± 35 Hz	150 baud Chan. Spacing 340 Hz FSK ± 70 Hz
1	425	680
2	595	1020
3	765	1360
4	935	1700
5	1105	2040
6	1275	2380
7	1445	2720
8	1615	3060
9	1785	
10	1955	
11	2125	
12	2295	
13	2465	
14	2635	
15	2805	
16	2975	
17	3145	
18	3315	

Table 9-3/Western Electric Operating Frequencies

signal are likely to vary and a sharper type of filter and wider bandwidths per channel are desirable to prevent serious interchannel interference.

FDM Configurations and Features

Frequency division equipment comes in two forms — single or dual channel stand-alone units and multichannel multiplexer assemblies. Multichannel units consist of channel cards

Channel Number	110 baud Chan. Spacing 170 Hz FSK ± 42.5 Hz	200 baud Chan. Spacing 340 Hz FSK ± 85 Hz
1	425	510
2	595	850
3	765	1190
4	935	1530
5	1105	1870
6	1275	2210
7	1445	2550
8	1615	2890
9	1785	
10	1955	
11	2125	
12	2295	
13	2465	
14	2635	
15	2805	
16	2975	
17	3145	
18	3315	

Table 9-4/MIL STD 188B Operating Frequencies

(which contain modulators and demodulators) and power supply elements. A common card bridges the individual channel cards to the line and provides a means of both adjusting the overall send signal level and distributing the receive signal. Most FDM units are designed to minimize the probability of a failure that would disable all the channels; putting power supply rectifiers and regulators on each channel card is one of the most effective methods to reduce the chances of such a failure. Single-channel units resemble modems in size and function and can be bridged onto the common line in a manner similar to the way modems are used in a polling system.

Each card in an FDM system must be programmed for the mark and space frequencies at which it is to operate. In some older systems it was necessary to have a different card for each channel; therefore, the cost of keeping spare channel cards on site was exorbitant. This problem has been solved in various ways. Plug-in frequency-sensitive elements make it possible to vary just a few components rather than the entire card. In other units, a change in channel position or data rate (while keeping the same family) requires only changing plug-in diode, resistor, or wire matrices. A most sophisticated technique controls all the channel parameters via digital counters and filters and is, therefore, fully strap programmable. Heterodyning techniques permit a fixed tuned discriminator to be used in all types of channels.

Channel interfaces commonly used with FDM are similar to those already discussed for TDM — namely, current loop, EIA RS-232, CCITT V.24, and MIL STD 188B. Control signal definitions and cable interfaces are as described in a later chapter. Strapping for controlled or continuous carrier operation is provided on a per-channel basis to facilitate the use of FDM equipment in polling systems. FDM systems are usually arranged so that the fastest channels requiring the widest bandwidths are assigned to the center of the band, with the slower channels on the sides. This technique minimizes the effects of line nonlinearities.

FDM Systems Applications

Figure 9-1 shows the major ways in which frequency division equipment can be used. The networks are either point-to-point or multipoint. If polling is used in a multipoint system, it is possible to use the same frequency channel for more than one channel. FDM and TDM may also be combined. FDM is used to collect the data from locations with only one

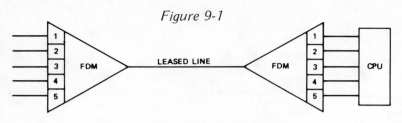

Figure 9-1

(a)/Point-to-Point FDM System

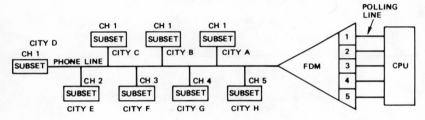

(b)/Multidrop FDM System with Polling

or two channels; all the FDM outputs then are remultiplexed via TDM for the long haul (Figure 9-2). It is expected that the TDM manufacturers will eventually offer FDM channel cards so that it is no longer necessary to have completely separate TDM and FDM units.

FDM Advantages and Disadvantages
The good news first — FDM systems are inherently speed adaptive. If a channel is programmed for 300 baud, it will work just as well at any slower speed, such as 134.5, 110, 75 or 50 baud, and this adaptability is not dependent on special characters or elaborate software. (Of course, this adaptive speed capability is not very efficient since bandwidth is wasted when a channel is used at a slow rate.) Having little common circuitry, FDM system failures usually affect just a single channel; since such failures are clearly assignable, repairs can be accomplished quickly. Economically, FDM can

109

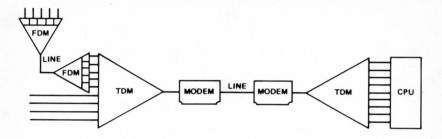

Figure 9-2/Combination of FDM and TDM may be more cost effective than either technique alone.

not be beaten where widely scattered synchronous terminals are to be collected and multiplexed. The cost of the common logic in TDM systems makes it impractical to pick up a single channel in a multipoint network. FDM units are inherently frame synchronized, so it is virtually impossible for demultiplexed data to be misdirected. Also, since no characters need be buffered, multiplexing delay is negligible. Frequency division multiplexers do not require modems to operate on analog lines, and therefore are easier to install and maintain. The bad news includes the fact that FDM is limited to the multiplexing of relatively low-speed start-stop data. The normal upper limit for an FDM multiplexer is 600 bps, although one can use a 202 modem with a 150 baud secondary channel as a cost-effective 1200 bps frequency division multiplexer. FDM is an analog technique and line noise, nonlinear frequency response, frequency translation, and harmonic distortion result in distortions in the recovered data that may cause errors. Some FDM units contain circuitry to regenerate data and clean it up, but such processing increases the cost; for TDM users, those capabilities are inherent and therefore free. FDM units can transmit only one control signal (Carrier On-Off) and thus are harder to interpose in auto-originate or auto-answer dial-up networks. A potentially serious drawback for the future is the fact that FDM units are not compatible with the new digital networks such as DDS. Where large capacity is required, FDM is found wanting. At 110 baud, FDM is limited to 20 channels, TDM to 118 (on voice-grade lines or DDS at 9600 bps); at 300 baud, FDM can handle 6 channels while TDM can pack in 38.

10

Turnabout Is Fair Play

INVERSE MULTIPLEXING

Most of this book is devoted to those devices that take many and make them fewer. Now we are considering some devices that take one and make it many. An inverse multiplexer takes a single serial data stream and divides it into two or more slower serial data streams. Why would anyone want to do such a thing? The train analogy can help here. Let us assume that so much freight has to be carried between two points that a continuously running train on a single track would have to run at 100 miles per hour. As Amtrak has learned, the cost of constructing and maintaining safe high-speed tracks is prohibitive. Thus in order to carry the load, a second track is commandeered, and the boxcars of freight are alternated between two trains, each running at 50 miles per hour.

Like fast tracks, wideband data lines are expensive. There is usually a long wait for them and they are not available in some areas. In addition, at the present time only 56 and 230.4 kbps lines are available from the Bell System in the United States. Since the highest data rate on voice-grade lines is 9600 bps, the gap between 9.6 kbps and 56 kbps is a large and costly one. The gap can be filled by an inverse multiplexer operating at 19.2 kbps over two 9.6 kbps lines.

Basic Inverse Multiplexer Configuration
Figure 10-1 illustrates how the inverse multiplexer fits into the system between a fast terminal and two phone lines. While our discussion is limited to two lines, the same techniques have been used to construct inverse multiplexers using 3, 4, or n transmission lines (n-plexing). All the inverse multiplexers commercially available at present are bit-interleaved, although there is no overpowering technical reason why this must be so. In any case, the bits from the terminal or CPU are alternated between the channels for transmission and then coalesced in the proper order at the other end.

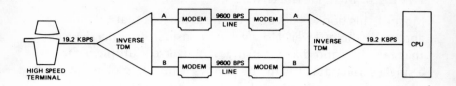

Figure 10-1/Basic Two-Channel Wideband Inverse Multiplexing System

This process seems simple, but because of the nature of transmission lines and clocking configuration problems, the logic required in such devices is quite complex. It is easy enough to alternate the bits on the two lines, but real telephone lines introduce substantial delay, and no two lines have exactly the same delay. What if the second bit arrives before the first bit or after the third, fifth, and seventh bits? Some typical line delay figures may help to indicate the magnitude of the problem. The period of a bit at 19.2 kbps is 50 microseconds. The delay in one mile of 22-gauge twisted pair is about 34 microseconds. A single L carrier link can introduce as much as 5.6 milliseconds of delay and a satellite link, hundreds of milliseconds. Since line delays are subject to drift with temperature, time of day, traffic load, etc., the inverse multiplexer must provide some means to measure the initial delay and then continuously track and correct for subsequent drifting. A practical inverse multiplexer can cope with as much as 800 milliseconds of differential delay between two transmission paths.

An error-protected alignment pattern is sent over the link to establish the existing difference in delay of the two paths. The data on the channel arriving first is shunted into a shift register and delayed until the corresponding bits of the alignment pattern appear on the other line. The composite data stream can then be assembled by alternating bits directly from the late line and from the proper stage of the shift register. Drift compensation is accomplished after alignment by counting clock cycles and adjusting the delay in the register whenever a clock pulse is gained or lost in one channel that is not gained or lost in the other. Using this technique, retrain cycles only need to be performed when the system is initiated, the data rate is changed, loopback tests are run, etc. The disadvantage of this technique is that, should a clock glitch occur, data will be garbled but the misaligned condition will not be detected or corrected until the terminal or computer sounds an alarm. The insertion of occasional sync bits to permit positive monitoring of the bit alignment are features of the more sophisticated units. The sync bits inserted are deleted from the data output and so the data throughput is very slightly reduced.

Clocking an Inverse Multiplexer System
Clocking is probably the most complex aspect of inverse multiplexing. Figure 10-2 shows one end of the system in detail. While the entire system could be timed by a station clock or a clock within the multiplexer, it is often the practice to derive all the clocks necessary at each end from one of the modem clocks. This method guarantees that the clock will meet the rather stringent requirements of the typical 9600 bps modem. For enhanced reliability, though, the system is designed to get its clock from the other modem in the event of a clock failure. This capability requires that the modems used be electronically switchable between the internal and external clock modes. The 19.2 kbps terminal and CPU send clocks are obtained by doubling the master modem clock. The data receive clock is generated by doubling either one of the modem receive data clocks. Control signals for the terminal or CPU are generated by "anding" the equivalent signals of the two modems.

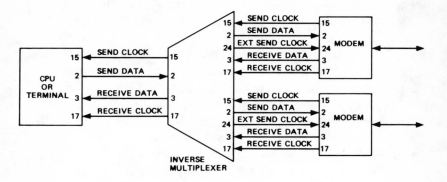

Figure 10-2/Clocking System Used in a Typical Inverse Multiplexing System

Other Uses of Inverse Multiplexers

If 7200 bps modems are used in a system such as illustrated in Figure 10-1, a data rate of 14,400 bps is obtained. As a matter of fact, most inverse multiplexers can operate with any combination of 9.6, 7.2, 4.8, 2.4 or 0 bps modems, permitting composite data rates of 19.2, 17.8, 14.4, 12.0, 9.6, 7.2, 4.8, or 2.4 kbps. The bits in mixed-speed systems are of course alternated in the proportions required.

Another useful application for the inverse multiplexer is in diversity transmission. In this application, both channels transmit the same data and the received data is taken from the line with the best signal quality. This application really does not require the facilities of an inverse multiplexer since no interleaving is involved, but such units do make provision for this mode of operation.

Automatic Fallback Features of Inverse Multiplexers

The inverse multiplexer capability of operating with a variety of unequal modem rates makes it possible to implement several automatic fallback modes. All these modes depend on

116

the ability of the modem to detect when the transmission line quality is not up to standard. Either the signal quality lead (pin 21) or carrier detect (pin 8) can be used to trigger these fallback mechanisms. For example, if signal quality drops on one line, all the data is shunted to the still good line and the data rate clock to the terminal is automatically reduced to that of the single still-operative modem.

If the modem data rate can be controlled via the pin 23 data-rate selector lead, it is possible to reduce the throughput on one or both channels electronically in response to an adverse line condition. Restoral can likewise be automatic. Unfortunately, automatic fallback and particularly automatic restoral have many pitfalls. Each time the data rate is changed, the multiplexers must inform the other end of the change and must go through a realignment cycle.

Before a realignment can be attempted, however, the modems must re-equalize. In a real system, signal quality may vary a great deal due to fading or noise, and a lot of transmission time and data may be lost due to frequent oscillation between the normal and the fallback states. Manual switches and straps can inhibit these functions and stabilize the system while adjustments or repairs are made.

Combining Multiport Modems and Inverse Multiplexers

If only 12, 14.4, or 17.8 kbps are used by the inverse multiplexer but two 9.6 kbps modems are installed anyway, the excess bandwidth can be used for other terminals or TDM's if one or both of the modems are equipped with the split-stream feature described in Chapter 3. In this configuration, one modem of the pair must be capable of being externally clocked by the inverse multiplexer even though the split-stream channel interface is being used.

11

Put On a Happy Interface

EIA RS-232C AND THE MULTIPLEXER
The No Man's Land of Multiplexers

The Electronic Industries Association publishes a specification, designated RS-232C, governing the interface between data communications equipment, such as modems, and data terminal equipment, such as teletypes and computers. Unlike some attempts at industry-wide standardization, this specification has been widely accepted, and virtually all American equipment manufacturers adhere to it with varying degrees of rigor.

There are two parts to RS-232. One specifies the electrical characteristics of the signals crossing the interface; the other, the connector pin numbers and the functions of these signals. The electrical characteristics are summarized briefly as follows: The interface signals may be either positive or negative with an absolute voltage of 3 to 25 volts. Signals between +3 and -3 volts are not defined. If a signal is data, then a mark is defined as negative voltage and a space as positive. If the line is a control signal, then the function is on when the voltage is positive and off when it is negative. In synchronous channels, the negative going edges of clock signals correspond to the center of the data bits. The interface lines are not damaged if accidentally shorted to ground or each other and the recommended load impedance is 3000 to 7000 Ω. The EIA interface is limited to cable runs of up to 50 feet (although hundred-foot lengths are quite commonly used without ill effect) and to data rates not exceeding 20,000 bps.

Table 11-1 lists the RS-232 interface signal leads that are of interest to us in this chapter. Note that if a signal is an output from a modem, it must be an input to a terminal. The specification is designed in regard to pin numbers so that a straight wire cable connecting identical pin numbers of a terminal and a modem always connects and matches inputs to outputs. Another definition that is implicit in the specification is the meaning of "Receive Data" and "Send Data." In

[Listed in order of appearance at computer]

EIA Pin #	Name of Signal	Abbr.	EIA Name	Direction	Function
22	Ring Indicator	RI	CE	to computer	indicates that phone is ringing
20	Data Terminal Ready (on)	DTR	CD	to modem	tells modem to answer call
6	Data Set Ready	DSR	CC	to computer	modem has answered & sent answer tone
8	Data Carrier Detect	DCD	CF	to computer	carrier tone present; o.k. to look at data
4	Request to Send	RTS	CA	to modem	tells modem to send carrier
5	Clear to Send	CTS	CB	to computer	o.k. for computer to send data
20	Data Terminal Ready (off)	DTR	CD	to modem	tells modem to hang up and end call

[Listed in order of appearance at terminal]

EIA Pin #	Name of Signal	Abbr.	EIA Name	Direction	Function
20	Data Terminal Ready (on)	DTR	CD	to modem	allows modem to remain off-hook
6	Data Set Ready	DSR	CC	to terminal	indicates dialing is finished
4	Request to Send	RTS	CA	to modem	tells modem to send carrier
5	Clear to Send	CTS	CB	to terminal	o.k. for terminal to send data
8	Data Carrier Detect	DCD	CF	to terminal	o.k. for terminal to receive data
20	Data Terminal Ready (off)	DTR	CD	to modem	tells modem to hang up and end call

[Other signals]

EIA Pin #	Name of Signal	Abbr.	EIA Name	Direction	Function
25	Out of Service	OOS		to modem	makes modem look busy to central office
15	Transmit Clock		DB	to terminal	clocks data from terminal
17	Receive Clock		DD	to terminal	clocks data to terminal
24	External Modem Clock		DA	to modem	clocks data to modem
2	Send Data	SD	BA	to modem	
3	Received Data	RD	BB	to terminal	

Table 11-1

a modem, received data (pin 3) is that which the modem is receiving from the telephone line and demodulating, not what it is receiving from the terminal. Transmit or send data (pin 2) is what the modem is modulating and transmitting down the telephone line, rather than that which it is sending to the terminal. From the terminal's point of view, receive data is what it receives from the modem; transmit data is what it sends to the modem.

What happens when a time division multiplexer is interposed in a system using terminals and modems (Figure 11-1)? If all terminals being multiplexed are within 50 feet of the multiplexer, they can be directly connected to the TDM and the multiplexer should look like a modem as far as pin numbers and control signals are concerned. The required interface is shown in Figure 11-1 for a dedicated half-duplex asynchronous terminal. But what if some of the terminals being multiplexed are remotely located, or dial-up and connect to the multiplexer via modems? In that case, the multiplexer must look like a terminal to the modem as far as pin numbers and control signals are concerned. Obviously, a single type of channel card for a multiplexer cannot look like a modem at one place and a terminal somewhere else. Different channel cards could be used to interface a particular channel to a modem or a terminal. This approach, however, has generally been rejected by the TDM manufacturers as impractical because of its cost and the obsolete inventory it leaves with the user as a system evolves. One common way to solve the problem is to make adapter cables that twist each input-output pair (Figure 11-2). But which interface should be twisted and which should use the straight cable? The EIA specification is of no direct help here, but it does specify that modems be equipped with a female 25-pin receptacle to accept a male cable from the terminal. The result is that virtually all terminals and computer ports come already outfitted with cables. It is therefore most logical and economical to make multiplexer inputs look like modems so that terminal cables

121

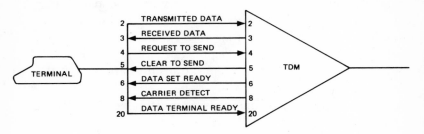

Figure 11-1/Interface Leads Between a Multiplexer and a Half-Duplex Asynchronous Terminal. The multiplexer appears to be a modem to the terminal.

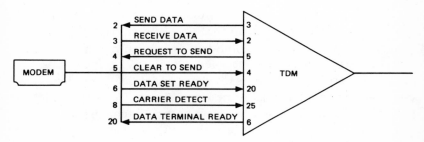

Figure 11-2/A twisted cable can make the TDM channel card of Figure 11-1 appear to be a terminal instead of a modem.

may be plugged in directly. The alternative would require that an adapter be used at the end of every terminal cable. Conversely, since modems do not come with cables attached, those required may just as well contain whatever twists are required and be furnished by the TDM manufacturer. This twisted-cable approach works, but in the absence of standards, each brand of multiplexer may require a different cable. This outcome results from the arbitrary pairing of inputs and outputs in the absence of a standard. It is logical to twist data pins 2 and 3 and perhaps 6 and 20 ("Data Terminal Ready" and "Data Set Ready") but should "Carrier Detect" be paired with "Busy Out" or "Request to Send"? What happens in multiplexers that transmit only two control signals rather than 3 or 4, with the choice of which two dependent on the application? Further complications become apparent when synchronous clock signals are considered and because of the differences between full-duplex and half-duplex terminals or modems.

Another disadvantage of the twisted cable approach arises with panel nomenclature. If a particular input signal lamp on a channel card displays "Data Terminal Ready" when a terminal is multiplexed and the panel is so labelled, then when a modem is connected to the same channel card via a twisted cable, the lamp does not show "Data Terminal Ready" but something else — perhaps "Data Set Ready" — and the labelling is incorrect. Therefore, the channel cards of some multiplexers are simply labelled "Send (or Receive) Control Signals 1, 2, 3, and 4," and the user must translate the numbers into the signals they represent according to whether a terminal or modem is attached. Other solutions to this problem include channel card switches, plugs, replaceable panels, overlays, etc.; they can eliminate the need for a twisted cable or neutral panel marking.

Simulating the EIA Handshake

In order for terminals to communicate via modems and phone lines with computers or other terminals, certain control signals must be transmitted in addition to data. These signals are defined fully in EIA RS-232, but a brief tabular review is included here for convenience. Table 11-1 lists the signals in the order they appear for the most complex case, in which a terminal calls a computer via two 202 modems using the switched network.

The first half of Table 11-1 lists the signals from the viewpoint of the answering computer; the other half, from the
originating terminal's viewpoint. Not every terminal and
computer looks at or generates all these signals, but those
signals that are used must either be transmitted between
multiplexers or provided locally. Figure 11-3 shows a directly connected terminal being multiplexed and eventually being directly connected to the computer. It is assumed that
both terminal and computer worked over the dial network
before the decision to multiplex was made and that the multiplexer chosen only comes with modem-like pin numbers.
One of the major savings in going to the TDM system is the
elimination of the pair of 202 asynchronous half-duplex modems formerly required on each channel (Figure 1-1). Therefore, both the terminal and computer — which have remained
unaltered — must be fooled into thinking they are still on the
dial network. The computer must see "Ring Indicator," and
both terminal and computer must see "Data Set Ready,"
"Carrier Detect," and "Clear to Send." Figure 11-3 shows
how, with special cables or channel card jumpers, this "de-
ception" may be accomplished using the fewest control signal paths and assuming identical modem-like TDM channel
cards at both ends of the system. The looping of "Request
to Send" to produce "Clear to Send" at the remote multiplexer insures that no data is sent before the other end has
been primed to receive it by "Carrier Detect." Figure 11-4
illustrates what is required if a full duplex leased-line extension circuit is interposed between the terminal and the TDM
in a system that was originally dial-up; Figure 11-5 illustrates
a dial-up extension circuit interface. Several additional EIA
cable configurations for synchronous terminals and modems
are illustrated in Chapter 3.

Transmission of Control Signals via Multiplexers

As indicated, the multiplexing of half-duplex terminals or
modems requires the transmission of control signal data
from one multiplexer to another over the trunk facility connecting them. There are several techniques available to carry
out this transmission; we now discuss the advantages and disadvantages of each.

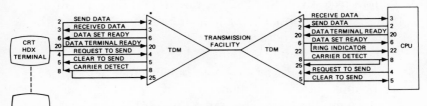

Figure 11-3/A possible interface between TDM's and half-duplex asynchronous terminals makes the multiplexer look like a dial-up modem to the terminals.

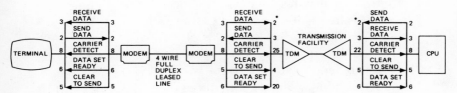

Figure 11-4/Control signal transmission and cabling in a full-duplex low-speed channel connected via modems to a TDM.

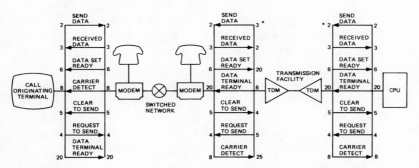

Figure 11-5/Control Signal Transmission and Cabling to Multiplex a Dial-Up Half-Duplex Terminal

Control signals may be thought of as very slow-speed digital data whose timing is asynchronous and random. Changes in control signals should be multiplexed and demultiplexed without excessive delay lest the turnaround time in half-duplex systems be unduly lengthened. False changes in control signals should be guarded against, since they could cause disconnections in dial-up systems and lost data.

Control signals must be coded in some manner before they can be multiplexed, and there are as many coding schemes as there are multiplexers. The state of each of the control signals is usually represented by one bit of a character known as a control word. The number of bits in a control word depends on the number of control signals being multiplexed and the character size used in the high-speed frame. Some multiplexers reduce the number of bits required or detect transmission errors by taking advantage of the fact that not all control signal states are possible. For example, in normal systems it is impossible to have "Carrier Detect" or "Clear to Send" on if "Data Set Ready" is off; to have "Ring Indicator " and "Carrier Detect" on simultaneously; or to have "Request to Send" without "Data Terminal Ready." These forbidden combinations are sometimes used for other control purposes, such as remote loopback, channel card testing, etc.

Nevertheless, whatever the code used to package such control data, only a few methods are useful in multiplexing control characters. Control characters may be multiplexed either in-channel or out-of-channel. In the freight train analogy, "out-of-channel" means that control characters are loaded in specially reserved boxcars, never in the same boxcars as data characters. It is therefore not necessary to label them, since their presence in the special boxcar means they are control characters. However, this technique is not effective in multiplexing because making the train longer decreases efficiency. In addition, if control characters from many channels share the same special boxcar, each character shipped must have an address label, which increases handling costs. Furthermore, there is always a possibility that data may be unloaded from the front of the train and lost before the car bearing the associated control information has been off-loaded and its contents sorted for delivery. In the in-band approach, data and control signals share the same freight-car position in subsequent trains but never ride together on the same train. The loading rules are quite simple in this approach — if there is no data to ship, load a control character. No freight car ever makes a trip empty. Since data is not normally transmitted anyway when signals such as "Data Set Ready," "Carrier Detect," "Clear to Send," and "Data Terminal Ready" are off, there is usually an overwhelming number of empty boxcars available to send control information, and a change in a control signal would reach the demultiplexer before the first data character. To protect against error, most TDM's require that two identical and bona fide control characters be received before any interface signals are altered.

The major drawback of the in-band control character technique is the need to distinguish between data and control characters, since they occupy the same freight car position. The most common marking technique is to have each control character preceded by a mark or space, depending on whether the character is data or control. Other bit positions or several bits per character may be used in a similar manner. The advantage of using only the first bit is that it is not necessary to wait for all the bits of a character to be received to know whether the character is data or control; this attribute can be used to shorten the demultiplexing time, particularly in bit-interleaved multiplexers. The major disadvantage of this technique is that one extra bit per character must be used even when data is being transmitted, reducing the efficiency of the multiplexer. For instance, six bits are required to transmit Baudot code data rather than just 5, 8 bits are needed for IBM, and 9 for ASCII codes. In the latter two cases there is a way to regain the lost efficiency. Both standard IBM- and ASCII-coded data are parity-protected codes.

127

The last bit of the IBM character is an odd-parity bit; the last bit of ASCII-coded data is, normally, an even-parity bit. Therefore, if control characters were generated with reverse parity in the last bit position, it would be possible to operate with 7- and 8-bit character sizes for IBM and ASCII data, respectively, resulting in enhanced maximum efficiency. All the in-band control signalling techniques have the very minor drawback that under noisy line conditions, data characters with wrong parity or identifying bits may be deleted, and distorted control characters may be outputted as data.

Even if the EIA control signals are not required, as with current loop terminals, such line conditions as all marks or all spaces and test signals require special control characters to transmit and must be distinguishable from normal data.

Synchronous Channel Control Signal Transmission

Normally, only half-duplex synchronous terminals require true end-to-end control signal transmission. When required, these signals may be sent out-of-band or in-band. Out-of-band signalling is usually quite inefficient, since control signal delay must be minimized for modems using such features as new sync or other fast turnaround techniques, and short delay implies many extra freight cars on the train.

In-band signalling is made possible by taking advantage of the fact that when control signals are off, data is not transmitted and the synchronous data line is marking. By detecting an abnormally long period of marks and then generating a character representing the state of the control signals, it is possible to transmit control information in-band and yet maintain full synchronous data transparency.

Other Data Communications Interfaces

Multiplexers must be flexible enough to interface to all the common terminals, modems, and computers. In recent years, several new interface standards have been proposed or introduced. Among these are the Bell System Digital Data System

Put On a Happy Interface

(DDS) interfaces, the Standard RS-449 (proposed by the EIA to replace RS-232), and the older Bell Wideband 303-type interface. Since a really useful multiplexing system must be able to cope with all of these carrier facilities, their important features are detailed below for reference.

Multiplexing 303 Wideband Terminals

Terminals designed to operate at such speeds as 50 kbps or 230.4 over phone company lines equipped with 303-type data sets must use a 12-pin Burndy coaxial connector (MD12MXP-17TC). The connector on the modem or multiplexer is the MD12MXR-8T. Coaxial cable is required to carry all data and clock signals; cable lengths are usually limited to 50 feet. The leads and their meanings are as follows:

Burndy pin no.	Name of Signal	Abbr.	Direction	Function
C	Clear to Send	CS	to computer	o.k. for computer to send data
D	Send Request	SR	from computer	normally strapped on; if off, marks only are sent
E	Send Data	SD	from computer/ TDM	
F	Data Set Ready	DSR	from modem	
G	Local Test	LT	from computer/ mix	initiates local loopback to computer or TDM
H	External Send Clock	SCTE	to modem	permits CPU or TDM to clock modem
J	Internal Send Clock	SCT	from modem	permits modem to clock CPU or TDM
K	Receive Data	RD	from modem	
L	Receive Clock	SCR	to computer	clocks receive data into CPU or TDM
M	AGC Lock	AGC	to computer	indicates weak line signal

129

A "marking" or control signal "off" condition is represented by no current flow (less than 5 ma into 100 ohms). A "spacing," control "on," or binary "0" condition is represented by a current of more than 23 ma into 100 ohms.

A "Data Terminal Ready" signal is also sometimes put on the shield lead of the M pin. This signal is at RS-232 voltage levels and has the RS-232 function of permitting the automatic answering of calls. It is mentioned here only to insure that the M shield lead is not shorted to ground by accident. The 303 modem is almost always strapped to ignore this signal. As noted above, the 303 wideband interface is quite similar to the leased line synchronous data interface discussed earlier. Due to the expense and difficulty of using the Burndy connector and the introduction of 56 kbps DDS service, this interface is expected to decline in use.

Digital Data System (DDS) Interfaces

At data rates of 2.4, 4.8, or 9.6 kbps, connecting a terminal or a TDM to the DDS is like connecting a synchronous terminal to a leased line synchronous modem. A DDS Data Service Unit (DSU) adheres to the EIA RS-232 specification and is equipped with the standard 25-pin connector. At 56 kbps, however, a 34-pin connector (Winchester MRA-34-P-JTC6-H8 or equivalent) is used at the end of the terminal cable and a balanced line driver and receiver permit up to 100 feet of cable to be used between the units. The signal on the line goes from +.55 volts to -.55 volts in going from "0" to "1". The pin assignments are given below. The definitions and voltages of the control signals are identical to those of the RS-232 interface. The major difference is that two leads rather than one are required for all data and clock signals.

Pin	Function	Direction
A	Protective Ground	—
B	Signal Ground	—
C	Request to Send	to DSU
D	Clear to Send	from DSU
E	Data Set Ready	from DSU
F	Receive Signal Detector	from DSU
R	Received Data	from DSU
T	Received Data	from DSU
V	Receive Data Clock	from DSU
X	Receive Data Clock	from DSU
P	Send Data	to DSU
S	Send Data	to DSU
Y	Send Data Clock	from DSU
a	Send Data Clock	from DSU

The phone company also offers a second way to connect the DDS, by hooking up directly to a Channel Service Unit (CSU). The DSU discussed above performs coding and decoding of data signals, clock recovery, and synchronization, generation and detection of control signals, EIA or balanced line interfacing, and all the functions of a CSU. A CSU essentially couples the data signals to the phone line and contains circuits which permit the phone company to initiate line checks from the central office.

It is expected that terminal, computer, and multiplexer manufacturers will provide built-in circuitry directly compatible with the DDS via the simpler, lower-cost CSU. This situation is similar to the analog line case where the phone company provides either a complete modem or a less expensive data access arrangement to which a customer-provided modem may be attached. The leads to the CSU are as follows (a 15-pin cinch DAMA-15-P cable is used):

Pin	Function	Direction
1	Ground	—
2	Status Indicator	from CSU
3	Received Data	from CSU
4	Received Data	from CSU
5	Send Data	to CSU
6	Send Data	to CSU

The status indicator signal is at RS-232 signal level and is similar to "Data Set Ready." The voltage on the data pairs is less than .21 absolute volts for a "0" and 1.75 absolute volts for a "1." (The DSU converts binary data to ternary coded data.)

Interfacing a Multiplexer to the DDS

Since the DDS is synchronized on a nationwide basis from a single clock, no provision is made in either the DSU or CSU for external clocking. Similar to the synchronous multiplexing systems discussed earlier, only one master clock per system can be tolerated. Therefore, even the largest DDS subscribers must slave their systems to the DDS clock; one way of doing so is illustrated in Figure 11-6. A problem arises only when an analog aggregate channel is being used to multiplex a variety of low-speed data sources, one of which happens to be connected to the TDM via a DDS tail circuit. If the aggregate line is also a DDS channel, no clocking problem exists because all the DDS clock rates are synchronized to each other. As shown in Figure 11-6, the DDS channel clock is used to synchronize an oscillator which provides the clock for the aggregate stream modem and multiplexer. Alternatively, if the aggregate line can run at one of the DDS data rates, a single DSU can be ordered at one end just to provide a synchronous clock for the system. Indeed an entire TDM network could, in theory, be clocked throughout by clocks derived from the DDS. A special low-speed DDS channel card would be required since it has to accept an external send clock as well as an external receive data clock.

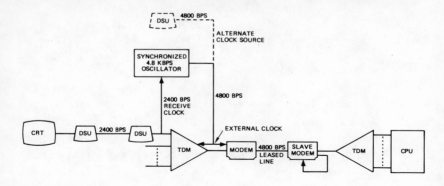

Figure 11-6/Multiplexing a DDS Channel onto a Non-DDS Leased Line

EIA Standard RS-449

A new EIA standard which is intended eventually to replace RS-232C has been drafted; it is likely that it will be formally adopted with little alteration. It has several advantages over the earlier standard. Principal among them is the ability to operate with cable lengths up to 200 feet at data rates to 20,000 bps using an unbalanced interface, and up to 2 mbps using a balanced line interface. Cable lengths longer than 200 feet should perform adequately at common data rates with either interface. The new RS-449, RS-422, and RS-423 define a new binary data interchange standard with new control functions and a larger 37-pin interface connector. The table below defines the signals in the new interface:

Additionally, pins 6, 8, 16, 20, and 21 are used as the second lead in the balanced interface for Send Clock, Receive Clock, External Clock, Send Data, and Receive Data, respectively. Pins 13, 15, 23, 25, and 28 are used for Secondary Channel, Receiver Ready, Clear to Send, Send Data, Receive Data, and Request to Send, respectively.

133

Pin No.	Function	Abbr.	RS-232C Equiv.	V.24 CCITT Equiv.	Direction
1	Send Circuit Ground	SC	—	—	—
2	Send Data	SD	BA	103	to modem
3	Received Data	RD	BB	104	from modem
5	Request to Send	RS	CA	105	to modem
7	Clear to Send	CS	CB	106	from modem
9	Data Mode	DM	DSR(CC)	107	from modem
10	Local Loopback	LL			to modem
11	Terminal in Service	IS	(busy out) (CF)		to modem
12	Receiver Ready	RR	Carrier Detect	109	from modem
14	Select Standby	SS			to modem
19	Receive Circuit Ground	RC			—
22	New Signal	NS	New Sync		to modem
24	Send Clock (Timing)	ST	DB	114	from modem
26	Receive Clock (Timing)	RT	DD	115	from modem
29	Terminal Ready	TR	DTR (CD)	108/2	to modem
30	Signal Quality	SQ	CG	110	from modem
31	Incoming Call	IC	Ring (CE) Indicator	125	from modem
32	Signalling Rate	SR	CH	111	to modem
33	Standby Indicator	SB			from modem
34	External Clock (Terminal Timing)	TT	DA	113	to modem
37	Test Mode	TM			from modem

RS-449 Connector Pin Functions

Put On a Happy Interface

The major new features of the interface, apart from electrical and mechanical differences, are the added control signals LL, IS, SS, NS, SR, SB, and TM. The circuit IS (In Service) is equivalent to the Busy Out or Out of Service signals used unofficially for some time; it causes a modem to look busy to an incoming call. The circuit NS is equivalent to the new sync feature used in some modems to permit a rapid resynchronization of the modem as soon as carrier appears after polling on a multidrop line. The signal SR (Signalling Rate) permits a modem to be switched from its normal data rate to an alternate rate by remote electronic means. The Local Loopback (LL) Signal permits a modem to be looped at its line side remotely by a terminal, computer, or multiplexer. The TM or Test Mode signal indicates that the modem has been placed in a test mode manually or via LL. SS (Select Standby) allows a modem to be switched electronically from one communications line to another, perhaps in response to an excessive error rate on the line. The Standby Indicator (SB) confirms that the modem has transferred itself to the standby facility.

The addition of these seven circuits to the seven already in common use will require a significant expansion in the control signal multiplexing capability of time division multiplexers. There could be as many as seven control signals used in each direction, requiring a seven-bit character to transmit, assuming those signals are kept as independent variables. The present 8- or 9-bit control words used in today's multiplexers will not suffice in this case. In the future, multiplexers with RS-449 compatibility will need more complex control signal logic and will require more circuitry on the channel cards to accommodate the extra signal receivers and drivers.

12

First Aid
for
Multiplexers

First Aid for Multiplexers

Multiplexers as System Troubleshooting Test Centers

There is no overwhelming reason why multiplexers should bear virtually the entire burden of testing and monitoring terminal, line, modem and computer port performance, yet such is traditionally the case. The buyer of a modern multiplexer gets not only a multiplexer but also an elaborate built-in multi-channel diagnostic test center. TDM manufacturers have taken their responsibility for testing quite seriously — to the extent that most TDM maintenance features are designed more to check the performance of the devices and lines being multiplexed than to monitor and test the multiplexer itself. In the following sections, an effort is made to sort out and categorize the various displays, switches, and alarms built into the modern TDM, and to show how they may be used to isolate system failure.

The basic purpose of all these test facilities is to enable even an unsophisticated user to isolate a problem in his system quickly, and either fix it himself or call on the proper serviceman. In a large system with equipment from many manufacturers, it is important to be able to identify precisely the source of difficulty, so as to avoid calling the wrong manufacturer's service center and incurring extra delay and cost. A plethora of lamps and switches, while sometimes initially confusing, makes it possible for relatively inexperienced personnel to isolate a failure in a system to a particular line or piece of equipment, just by reporting to a remote communications manager or manufacturer which lamps are lit, and by operating clearly labelled test switches. The operator of a multi-vendor communications system, with good user-oriented test features available to him, can usually find and correct failures and get back in operation faster than can the owner of a wholly common-carrier-supplied system totally lacking in user-operable diagnostics, where even the simplest test and repair procedures must be carried out by the carrier's technician in person on site.

Channel Monitoring Lamps

Since the invention of compact light-emitting diodes, which seldom burn out (and therefore rarely need replacement) and require no elaborate sockets, it has become practical to have continuous monitoring of all significant channel functions. In such displays the information is continuously presented and, usually, no interruption of normal data transmission is required to use them.

For full low-speed channel monitoring capability, the following signals should be displayed (although few multiplexers actually do have them all):

1. *Send Data*
2. *Receive Data*
3. *Send Clock (synchronous channels and trunk lines)*
4. *Receive Clock (synchronous channels and trunk lines)*
5. *Data Set Ready*
6. *Data Terminal Ready*
7. *Request to Send*
8. *Clear to Send*
9. *Ring Indicator*
10. *Busy Out*
11. *Carrier Detect*

In most multiplexers these lamps are located on the channel cards themselves; all channels can be observed simultaneously. A few multiplexers have one set of lamps which must be switched to the desired channel. The disadvantages of this method are that a failure common to all channels is not as readily apparent, general activity on the channels cannot be assessed at a glance, and the actual monitoring point is usually farther from the interface than is desirable. In regard to this last comment, it should always be remembered that if an output display lamp is not directly monitoring the output pin, there is a finite possibility that there is an interface failure beyond that point that the lamp cannot indicate.

A full set of signal monitoring lamps is often all that is required to find trouble quickly in many failure situations. A few examples serve to indicate how these lamps may be used to isolate a failure. In the system of Figure 12-1, the teletype operator complains that he is receiving data from the computer and that he is in a ready mode, but that the computer does not appear to acknowledge his transmissions. Other terminals in the multiplexer system are working normally. The lamps for the channel in question at both TDM locations are found to agree; they show that the data line is always marking and that carrier is off. All other lamps ("Data Set Ready," "Data Terminal Ready," etc.) are normal. Since the data flow in one direction is normal, the low-speed 2-wire line must be intact. The problem cannot be in the multiplexer, since the lamp displays at both ends agree and the lamp shows that the data from the terminal is not even reaching the multiplexer to be multiplexed. The failure, therefore, since not in line or TDM, is almost certainly in the remote 103 modem and,

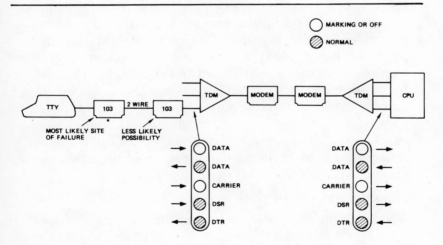

Figure 12-1/TDM channel card lamp display allows failure to be isolated to remote 103's.

most likely, is in its transmitter, although there is a slight possibility that both the demodulator and the "Carrier Detect" sections of the local 103 modem have failed simultaneously. If the carrier lamp were on, indicating the presence of "Receive Carrier" from the line, then the problem would have to be either in the remote 103 data modulator, the local demodulator, or the terminal transmitter. The standard and easily applied loopback tests of the modems and terminal would resolve these remaining ambiguities. For purposes of clarity, the possibility of cable failures in these examples is ignored. It always pays, however, to examine sockets and cables for signs of mechanical damage or looseness before resorting to more elaborate or costly diagnostic procedures.

If the terminal were not receiving data and "Carrier Detect" were also off, a line failure would be clearly indicated. Similar diagnosis is possible in dial-up situations. A terminal user complains that his calls to the computer are not answered. Observation of the channel card at the computer end of the system shows the presence of "Ring Indicator" but no response of a "Data Terminal Ready" signal from the computer to allow the modem to answer the call — clearly a computer front-end failure. Perhaps "Data Terminal Ready" is observed but is not seen at the other end of the system after demultiplexing. Ostensibly, the control signal has been lost in the multiplexer; probably a TDM channel card has failed. If other channels are working normally, it cannot be a trunk line, TDM central logic, or modem problem. If "Data Terminal Ready" is observed at both ends and the call is still not answered, the automatic answering feature of the modem or data access arrangement has failed.

Trunk Lamp Displays

When multiple channel failures occur simultaneously, a multiplexer or trunk facility problem is quite likely. A quick examination of the trunk data and carrier lamps can sometimes isolate the problem to the multiplexer common logic, the trunk modem, or the line. For example, the presence of "Trunk Carrier" in the absence of received data eliminates the line as a probable cause of the failure. Two additional diagnostic lamps found in almost all time division multiplexers indicate that the local TDM is out of frame sync or that the remote TDM is out of sync. The combination of these out-of-sync lamps, "Carrier Detect," and the data lamps makes trunk fault isolation that much easier. For example, if carrier is present and the data lamp shows that data is being received but the TDM is out of sync, then TDM failure is most probable, since either the local sync detection logic has failed or the remote TDM is not generating or outputting the proper sync character. An out-of-sync indication accompanied by no received data but good carrier indicates a modem failure. A failure of both remote sync and local sync accompanied by loss of carrier but not "Data Set Ready" almost certainly means a line failure, since it is unlikely that both sides of a modem would fail simultaneously and the possibility of modem power failure is eliminated by the presence of "Data Set Ready."

Loopback tests can further refine the diagnostic process, but it is the display lamps that indicate the results of the loopback tests and pinpoint the failure.

Loopback Diagnostics

The purpose of loopback testing is to isolate each element in a system from the next and loopback the system one level at a time until an open or faulty loop is found. Loopback features are best designed to allow an operator to test both ends of the system from whichever end he is at. Figure 12-2 shows 12 points of loopback which might be available in a typical system. Ideally, all of them should be possible, but the specific equipment purchased is the determining factor. Not all the loopbacks shown are under the control of the multiplexer. Numbers 3, 4, 5, and 6 are initiated at, and depend upon, the modem used. Numbers 9, 10, 11, and 12 depend upon

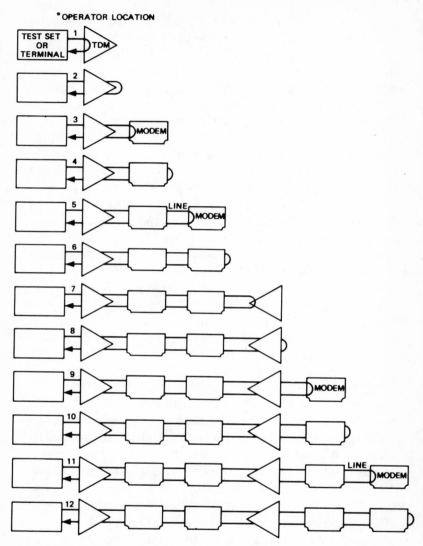

Figure 12-2/Twelve Possible Loopback Points in a Typical System Toward the Operator

both the modem and the multiplexer, since the loopback control signals must pass through the multiplexer to reach the remote modems. Therefore, the format of this control signal must be capable of being both multiplexed and recognized by the remote modems, usually necessitating that the remote low-speed modems and the multiplexer be from the same manufacturer. Use of multiplexers with built-in modems can also provide greater diagnostic control over these components than can external modems.

In diagnosing a failure, an operator activates each loop in succession, observing the appropriate lamp display, until an abnormal combination of lamps is observed. The assumption is that a test signal and/or control signals are being fed into the system so that there is something tangible to loopback and observe.

Figure 12-2 shows only loops back toward the operator. Most TDM's and modems also provide loops facing away from the operator, which are useful if two operators, one at each end, are available to activate the loopback switches for each other. Quite often where an operator cannot initate a loopback toward himself from some point in the system, a remote assistant can accomplish it for him. Figure 12-3 illustrates four common loops heading away from the operator that may be initiated by him to help a remote service technician who is electronically unable to loop these points himself.

Note that the loopback facilities shown assume a full-duplex four-wire system. In Figure 12-2 it is impossible to loop 103 modems as shown in loops 10 and 11, unless the transmitter frequency can be shifted to match the receiver frequency. This shift, however, reduces the effectiveness of the test, since the transmitter may loop but still not function in its normal frequency band. Another caveat to be remembered in looping a multiplexer on itself (as in loop 2 in Figure 12-2) is that the multiplexer is now running on its own internal clock. If the loopback test clock is much faster than

*OPERATOR POSITION

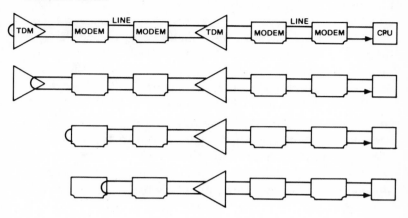

Figure 12-3/Four loopbacks away from an operator may assist a remote service technician to diagnose a problem.

that of the modem, it is difficult to test low-speed synchronous data channels or to check that the TDM has not been over-programmed to operate with too many low-speed channels. In synchronous systems, the master modem is best included in the loop; if the only included modem is a slave modem, the system may be left without a clock. In loop 3 (Figure 12-2), both send and receive data are normally clocked by the internal oscillator in the modem. If this clock is permanently disabled when the modem is strapped for external timing, then there will be no clock when the digital loopback switch on the modem is used. Loops 4 and 5 may likewise not operate properly, since a modem slaved to its own receive clock attempts to bootstrap itself into operation by using a clock recovered from its own receive data stream to synchronize data which is responsible for this received data stream, and so forth. Newer models contain circuits

144

which allow the internal clock to function when the external one fails or when no receive data transitions are detected. Therefore, with such a modem, loop tests 3, 4, and 5 are effective.

The better TDM's have lamps which indicate that a successful remote TDM channel or trunk loopback has been accomplished. Since these lamps are activated by control signal patterns that have made a complete passage around the loop, their being lit indicates that all modems and lines are reasonably intact and that most, if not all, of the TDM common logic is indeed functioning. Thus, if the low-speed channel loopback lamp is on, the problem almost surely lies beyond the remote multiplexer or in the interface portion of the channel card itself.

Built-In Test Character Generators and Error Detectors

Several TDM's have built-in test character generators that can be switched to any channel. The pattern is usually fixed and is not necessarily meaningful in all speeds or codes. However, built-in compare and error-detection circuits make it possible to use this convenient facility in conjunction with the remote loopback feature to refine the diagnostic procedure. Test characters can be fed into a variety of points in a multiplexer. For instance, one may be multiplexed in a given channel slot in place of local data, sent on a trunk line to a remote TDM, looped back at the remote channel card, multiplexed again, transmitted, and finally demultiplexed; then, any detected errors are displayed. Such a test catches failures that may not be downright catastrophic and that therefore would be hard to detect using the normal display lamps.

This diagnostic facility is brought into play manually when a failure is called to the operator's attention by a user. Other test character systems operate automatically and periodically on a per-channel basis and raise an alarm whenever a persistent error is detected. In a multiplexer lacking such a feature, it is possible to create one if the multiplexer is capable of transmitting control signals. For example, an unused control signal, such as "Send Ring Indicator," could be strapped on at one end of the system and looped back at the other. Should the returning ring indicator signal go off, it would show that an abnormal condition exists and constitute a failure alarm. In this case the test character is the control character used for "Ring Indicator." In several multiplexers this capability is already built in; it is not necessary to sacrifice a control signal.

In some multiplexers a local common logic monitoring function is continuously performed by multiplexing, demultiplexing, and comparing a test character in a phantom channel. A major advantage of this technique (or others for local common logic testing) is that the alarms so generated can be used to initiate an automatic switchover to an alternate set of common logic.

Parity and Sync Error Counters

While lamps and loopback switches make it easy to locate major hardware failures quickly, there are cases where nothing has failed but performance is degraded due to transmission line noise. Quite often line failures occur gradually, with error rates building up over a period of days. Sometimes error rates depend on the time of day because of phone company busy-hour interference problems. In any case, a trunk line error counter can be a valuable aid in detecting such problems.

The frame sync pattern in all TDM's is known and repeats periodically. Thus, a simple error detector with a counter and display can show a number that is proportional to the actual error rate on the line. If the counter can be made to decrement periodically, it is possible to have it continuously display the approximate excess error rate. In multiplexers whose trunk characters have parity, additional characters can be checked for errors. In some cases, such parity counters can be switched to a low-speed channel to check the error rate of the incoming data. One early multiplexer had the